The Journey of an Artist: Eric Lee

RONIN
ERIC LEE

Edited by Lady L. Reed & Joycelyne Lew

The Journey of an Artist:

Eric Lee

By Ronin and Eric Lee

Edited by Lady L. Reed and Joycelyne Lew

All rights reserved. Any portion of this book may not be reproduced or used in any manner without the permission of the publisher.

Copyright: 2020 Eric Lee

First Printing: 2020

ACKNOWLEDGEMENT

I'd like to say thank you to Ronin for helping me write this book, to Joycelyne Lew for proof reading and editing it, and to Lady L. Reed for all the work she did to make this book possible.

A special thanks to Al Dacascos, Dan Inosanto, Ernie Reyes Sr., Benny Urquidez, Bob Wall, Cynthia Rothrock, Don Wilson, Art Camacho, Michael Matsuda (Martial Arts History Museum), Dr. Rick Lengyel, Cindy Daoud, David L. Reed, and KW Wong for being my friend.

I also appreciate all my martial arts friends (too many to mention) and family who supports me all these years.

Most of all, I thank God for this great life.

FOREWORD

I have always had a high respect and have the fond memories of Eric Lee. He is truly a gifted martial artist and it seems to me that he always puts others before himself. We are truly blessed by having him in the Martial Arts community. He was always doing things for the good of martial arts community.

I've had the privilege of traveling with him when we toured Mexico for Martial Arts demonstrations at various cities. I have also had the privilege of traveling with him to England when we did demos there. He is definitely an ambassador of goodwill for all martial artists regardless of style, an expert on his own martial arts but willing to learn other martial arts to be well-rounded and open minded.

I am truly blessed by having him as a friend. The martial arts community needs more people like him.

Dan Inosanto

Eric Lee is one of the best martial artists I've ever met in my 66 years in martial arts. More importantly, Eric is a very good man, smart, kind, fun, ethical, and extremely talented. God bless my friend Eric Lee.

Respectfully,

Bob Wall

Grand Master Eric Lee is a living legend and I am honored to be able to call him my mentor and friend. He is definitely one of the pioneers of martial arts in America that dominated forms competitions. His book, "The Journey of an Artist", will not only reveal his mastery of martial arts but mastery of life.

I was honored as one of the greatest masters of the 20th century on TNT TV and I was awarded this title in the 1980's for producing 7-national forms champions in one year. George Chung was the #1 male forms champion, Cynthia Rothrock was the #1 female champion, and my son, Ernie Reyes Jr., was the youngest child ever to be rated in adults forms division making martial arts history at the age of 8 years old. My demonstration team, The West Coast Demo Team, was rated as the #1 demo team in the world. Eventually, we were discovered and did movie and television projects in Hollywood.

I am proud to say our accomplishments were greatly influenced by GM Eric Lee, who in the late 1970's, was known as the King of Kata or Forms. My champions helped revolutionized creative forms in America because we used dynamic music. At first, we were not accepted by the traditional masters. Even though we would not score high and win initially because music was radical at the time, we would get standing ovations from the audience. GM Eric Lee would be one of the judges and he was open-minded to score us the highest. I would go up to him, bow, then ask him, "Sir, how can we get better?" GGM Eric would always give positive advice and encourage us to keep being innovative.

Our performance success was the result of watching GM Eric do his solo performances with other legends of martial arts in America such as GM Tadashi Yamashita and GM Byong Yu. To see GM Eric perform was amazing! Dynamite does come in small packages! GM Eric, despite being small in stature he was unbelievably powerful, fast, and devastating martial artist! GM Eric was our role mode of excellence.

What impresses me most about GM Eric Lee is not only about his mastery of the martial arts, mastery of music and song but having a giant heart!

GM Eric Lee is one of the most caring, kind and giving human beings I have ever met! No doubt GM Eric's "The Journey of an Artist", is one of living the highest values of martial arts training of Honor, Loyalty, Family and Bravery!

Much Honor and Love!
Grand Master Ernie Reyes

Like most stunt guys, their names may not be as big as the main actors. Eric Lee is one of the pioneers of Kungfu who made it in films more or less like me.

Looking back in the past, he's been one of the loyal friends one can get over the years. He's not much into competition after 1973. He's shown me how life can be enjoyed too.

We are brothers in martial arts and entertainment industry.

Aloha!

Benny "Jet" Urquidez,

We are great friends. I haven't seen him in person lately, but we talk every now and then. It was a great pleasure for me to have work with him in a lot of projects, hang out with him, and even got to travel to China in one of his group travels. I was always so excited working with him in the past. When we see each other on events, we always have a good laugh. I will always remember him as the King of Kata. He's the fastest Kungfu guy back then after Bruce Lee. He's so exotic in his own ways. To finally read this book and have the honor of writing something for him definitely is my pleasure. Who wouldn't do anything for our friend, Eric?

- Cynthia Rothrock
  8th degree in Tang Soo Do, Blackbelt in TKD, Karate, Eagle Claw, Wushu, Northern Shaolin, Pai Lum Tao Kungfu, World Champion, multiple Martial Arts Hall of Fame Inductee in Martial Arts, actress

I met My Sifu Eric Lee, in the late 80's at a Kung Fu seminar he was conducting. Little did I know then that the "King of Kata", a martial arts master who had graced the covers of martial arts magazine worldwide, would be intertwined with my success in martial arts and films for the rest of my life. I wasn't the most skilled of his students nor the brightest, nor the best, but I did have the perseverance to stick with it. Sifu Eric Lee took me under his wing and mentored me in not only the art of Wun Hop Kuen Do, Kung Fu but in life.

He became more than a martial arts instructor to me, he became my family and has been a constant source of guidance and inspiration.

I witnessed firsthand the explosiveness that made him one of the greatest Kung Fu masters of his era and I witnessed the true compassion of his soul.

This book was long overdue as it is a blueprint to achieving happiness and inspiration through not only the martial arts but the journey and transformation. His story about a little kid from China reaching the greatest heights in Hollywood and becoming a part of some of the most iconic action motion pictures of our time is truly epic.

- Art Camacho: Award winning Film Director, Fight choreographer, Stuntman, Actor, author, Martial artist, and multiple Martial Arts Hall of Fame Inductee.

I have known Eric Lee since he was a Tournament competitor in the 70's. He is truly a phenomenal Martial Arts Competitor, as well as Actor, Fight Choreographer, Producer, Teacher, etc. But, my most extreme opinion of Eric is that, he has been a totally committed and loyal friend since we met. He is a "True" Grandmaster of Life not just the Martial Arts! I have admired and appreciated his friendship and all his positive contributions to my life. He was my first choreographer and worked on such films as "Ring of Fire", which probably had some of the best fight scenes of the times. I am giving his book "An Artist's Journey" my highest recommendation and can't wait to read it myself!!!

Sincerely your Friend,

Don "The Dragon" Wilson

I first met GM Eric Lee at a fight film audition in Hollywood, CA. two weeks before the Bruce Lee Collection Audition on Aug.7, 1993. We met, shook hands and we talked till the event was over. That day was one of the best in my life. He introduced me to many famous people, most I still know today. Upon leaving this event, I found my car was locked up at the bank gate. Eric Lee offered to give me a ride home. When we got to my house, I asked him in for some tea. I was so excited Eric Lee was at my house in Hollywood. He liked my home training gym and acupuncture books. We talked about martial arts, taichi, Qigong and his earlier career in films.

Two weeks later we met again at the Bruce Lee Auction. He introduced me to Linda and Shannon Lee and also Rev. Leo Fong, a student of Bruce Lee in Oakland. Little did I realize Rev. Leo Fong would be the Minister who married me to my wife Debra on Santa Monica Pier on July 28, 2005. Eric Lee was my best man.

As the year went on we stayed close friends. We even shared living in the same house for one month before Eric moved to Oakland, CA. I helped him move and we drove a big truck over the giant bridge into Oakland. I got to meet his father and sister then we left to drive over the Golden Gate Bridge to San Francisco to Chinatown for a nice dinner. The next day, I flew back to Los Angeles. What a great weekend with Eric Lee!

A few months later, I returned to my birth city, Pittsburg, PA to create my career as an acupuncture doctor. The years passed on and we saw each other often. We went to the "Arnold Classic", then I set up a seminar for him in the Pittsburg area. We last met in Las Vegas then Los Angeles 4 years ago. I saw a new side of GM

Eric Lee, his mind has grown more mature. New talent he was born with I began to see. He has the ability to do art quality work and play music on different instruments. The new side is coming out.

Now, four years later, this new talent is being developed and progressed. He is now singing, playing instruments, painting, calligraphy and much more.

I would like to thank Eric Lee for an exciting and a special lifetime that I will never forget, all the great times together.

Sincerely,
Dr. Rick Lengyel

(Martial Arts)

"Things have roots and branches; To know what precedes and what follows. Is nearly as good as having a head and feet." - Confucius

PROLOGUE:

"There was nothing I could do..."

Fu Chung Village, Canton, China

I stood in the morning sun, looking down the barrel of the soldier's rifle. I was only about 2 years old but I knew what a gun was, and I could see the hateful, angry look on the face of that soldier, under the brim of his uniform cap.

I don't know why the soldiers were there, or what side they were on... Or even if there WERE sides. Perhaps even their commanding officer didn't know that the soldiers were there, looting the countryside – to this day I don't know.

But in that moment I, Eric Wing Chow Lee, knew that my life hung in the balance, and that I was powerless to do anything to save myself... But thankfully, the soldier didn't pull the trigger.

I looked on, stunned and helpless as the soldiers ransacked our home, bullying and taking whatever they wanted. When they were done, the house was set on fire, and partially burned.

I couldn't understand what was happening, or why.

I had no way of knowing that a civil war was raging and that soldiers were in the final phases of a struggle for power to control the changes that lay ahead.

Mother & Eric

Nor did I know that only 4 years later, my whole world would change, or that I would be embarking on the first big step in my life's journey – a journey that would eventually give me a new name, in a new language that I had never even heard, and take me half a world away to a strange new country that I had never seen and never even knew existed; a journey that would take me all around the world, and raise me to superstar status in the international martial arts community.

My life could easily have ended that day, but it didn't.

I had no way of knowing it on that day, standing there, helplessly, looking up into the barrel of that soldier's gun, but I was to become someone the people still call, "Kung Fu's Little King of Kata."

You never know what life has in store for you.

(Love)

"The truly great man dwells on what is real and not what is on the surface. On the fruit and not the flower." - Lao Tzu

CHAPTER ONE: The Fire Within

— "I don't believe in 'fail.' I don't believe in 'succeed.' I don't believe in 'age': I believe in 'DO.'"

Hello. I'm Eric Lee, and this book is my legacy — my life story.

Hopefully, it's also my gift to you, because it's my hope that perhaps by sharing it with you, you can find something in these pages that in some way will make your life a little better. We can all use a bit more sunshine in our lives.

I don't know who you are, reading these words, of course, but I love what I do, and I love sharing what I do, so that's what I'm doing right now, at this very moment — Trying to provide some 'inspiration' before my 'expiration' —

Ok, maybe it's not the best play on words, but my sincere hope is that I can encourage you to find your own dreams, just as I did.

We are all here only temporarily, but I guess you could say if I can in some way inspire you, that's a kind of immortality. So I get something good out of this, too.

We're all each other's teachers. Each of us knows things the other person doesn't. Over my 72 years — that's the age I am now, as I write these words – my students in their own ways have taught me as much as I've taught them, and I'm hoping this book will do the same. My methods have worked for me – Perhaps you can "pick up" some of them, and they'll work for you too. If you like them and they make sense to you, then perhaps you'll share them with others who are interested.

That's my hope, and my reason for writing this.

I'm known primarily as a martial artist and a grandmaster of kung fu, but as we say in America, I also wear a number of other hats – actor, painter, calligrapher, author, executive producer of movies... I feel very fortunate for everything that life has brought to me. I count my blessings every day.

I see myself as an artist. Artists do what they love to do, and that's what I'm doing. I'm fortunate, because my body is still pain-free. Not everyone is as fortunate – and I'm grateful for that. I've always led a very healthy life, and thankfully, I can still do all of the things I did as a young man.

I'm still a martial artist of course... I retired from most teaching in 2009, but if a student came to me with the real desire to learn, I could still teach that student everything he needs to know... *But the one thing I cannot teach is the desire to learn – not just the desire to learn kung fu, but the desire to learn anything.*

That desire, that "fire within," is the one thing that cannot be taught.

I can't teach that. No one can. It has to come from a place deep inside yourself that only you have access to, and only you can listen to. And that's a profound secret:

I believe that the first key to discovering your own, personal path in life, is finding something that you REALLY want to DO. Something that you can immerse your whole BEING in. That's step one, and it's a big one.

None of us knows what that "something" is, until we trip over it in the course of living our life – we have to FIND it for ourselves. For me it was the martial arts... for others it may be computers, or mathematics, or herbs, or yoga, or music, or writing... It can be anything, big or small... it might change to something else over time... But it has to be something that motivates, something that fascinates, something that you absolutely can't get enough of.

> "Eric is fearless, and MOSTLY wise... He's got more energy than ANYBODY... His techniques are beyond anything I've ever seen - I'm mostly in awe of them and I'm not impressed by too many people.
>
> "He always has 1000 irons in the fire, and SOMEHOW, they all wind up getting done... And you find yourself saying, 'How the hell did he do it???' It's like magic."
>
> - Jin Quan, Natural Healer, Eric's longtime roommate in Los Angeles.

Having found that, you then have to discover not only the means to do it, but also the support of that pursuit.

Still, this is not a book of philosophy, although some may find practical philosophy in it. Similarly, it is not precisely a "biography" although it chronicles a life. It is not a "self-help" book, nor is it intended as a "training manual," or a "how-to" book, but hopefully, you may find some useful elements in these rambling pages, as well.

This is a book about inspiration. It is the story of one person's life-journey from a tiny village in China, to become one of the world's best-known martial arts "icons," and how he got there –

But I really didn't write it as some sort of "vanity project," or to celebrate or aggrandize myself and tell you what a great guy I am, or any such nonsense: I wrote it simply to say to future generations, "Look, this is what I did: If *I* can do this, **you** can do it too: If, from my humble origins, I can achieve MY dreams, so can you."

That's my purpose here.

This book is something I hope will encourage people to seize their life and take action. I'm just a guy from a small village in China. But I've come a long way with my philosophy of life. I am sharing it with others so that hopefully they can benefit from some of the things I discovered in the course of my life and be inspired to do the same.

What we think, matters. Our thoughts have power – real power. They literally shape the steps that we take through life, and over time, they can even affect such things as our physical health.

I spend a lot of time thinking strategically – not just creating random, warm and fuzzy thoughts that make me feel good, but thoughts that help me create an environment that is conducive to well-being and taking positive action.

My belief is that if we get good at this, we create a mindset that helps us free ourselves to achieve... and yes, a lifestyle that supports that mindset: It works for me! So I'm hoping that some of this philosophy may rub-off on you as well.

I see lots of self-help books on the market these days. But probably most of them just sit on the shelf and gather dust: The simple truth is that all the self-help books in the world, all the lifestyle gurus in the world cannot reliably teach one, single, fixed formula that is absolutely guaranteed to help you achieve success.

This is NOT a "self-help" book: I cannot give you a fixed formula or canned method for living your life. There is no formulaic "how to," for life. There is no fixed "way" that someone else can teach you. Inspiration has no canned formula. There is only "YOU CAN."

I can't tell you directly what you should do...

But I CAN tell you what *I* did, and hopefully give a few pointers – a few attitudes and ideas that have helped me along, and hopefully you can draw inspiration from that.

...And yet, if you look within these pages, you may well find words and thoughts that will light up new corners of your mind, or perhaps affirm and lend strength to ideas you've already had floating around inside your head; things that may help guide yourself in your journey along your own path in life. That is my hope for anyone who reads these words.

<u>The REALLY good news is that the Way of Life is discovered within, and we all possess the means to look within and discover it</u>.

I'm writing this book to try to give you the inspiration you need to help make that discovery for yourself.

That's my message to future generations. I hope it serves you as well as my life has served me.

(Creativity)

"The most beautiful thing we can experience is the mysterious." – Albert Einstein

CHAPTER 2: Discovering a Way of Life

"We are all the product of our own attention."

When I was a small boy, I certainly didn't know that Kung fu was going to inspire me as it did, or guide my footsteps through life... but the truth is that *we are all the product of our own attention*:

What we experience, think, see, and feel, through a truly mysterious process, guides what steps we will take through life, and determines what we will become. The first step determines the next. Life is like that.

You never really know what your True Path in life may be. It has to be discovered. Life is always lived one step "outside the box" – It's been my experience that to get creative, we have to get outside of our formality, get outside of our boundaries: I've learned to be aware of when I enter that space, and I've learned to be very comfortable in that place "outside the box."

We Chinese have a saying: "A turtle never goes anywhere unless he sticks his neck out." I believe that is true.

In a way, life is like the headlights on a car when you are drive at night – you can only see about 50 yards in front of you – you don't know every turn you're going to make to get to where you're going, but know where you want to wind up. So you have to be brave, and have faith that once the headlights get a little further down the road, there will be another 50 yards visible in the headlights –

I feel you have to trust the unknown in order to know, and not worry about the next 100 yards until you get there: Worry is a dividend you pay for adversity in advance.

Kung fu was always a part of my life, almost like a part of the furniture – it was always there in the background. It was there in the Chinese opera which my grandmother took me to see in Hong Kong, at about age 6 – she and I were close, and I loved her very much. She taught me a lot, and I enjoyed her company. She raised me for the most part.

Chinese opera is a popular, traditional form of drama and musical theatre that is very, very old in China. It features a wide variety of Chinese art forms... music, song and dance, acrobatics, costumes, masks... and naturally, all that included the martial arts. If you enjoy seeing Jackie Chan's moves, his background is Chinese Opera. I can't speak for him, of course, but I still see the Chinese Opera training in his movement.

Kung fu was there, too, when I watched my father as a young child, doing his Choy Li Fut kung fu style. I never trained with him, but I watched him train at an early age.

All those experiences of childhood are still with me, as they are with everyone. We experience them, not knowing what impact they will have on our lives, or where that aspect of our attention – what we think and feel about what we see – will lead us.

It eventually led me to study the martial arts.

There are many "styles" of the martial arts. There are styles that mainly involve grappling, there are styles that involve punching and striking with the hands, styles that center upon kicking, "soft styles," "hard styles," styles that use weapons... More than you can count. New ones that I've never heard of seem to crop up every day.

> "Eric Lee is one of the greatest martial artists of all time, and a great man."
>
> – Bob Wall – martial artist, actor – and the iconic character, "Ohara," in Bruce Lee's classic "Enter the Dragon."

But today, after more than half a century of being absolutely *immersed* in the martial arts, I don't believe in "styles" anymore – I have studied many. The martial arts, at least on the surface, are a study of fighting and self-defense: I've come to feel that there are certain anatomical targets and certain weapons, and logical, high-success strategies and principles for getting the weapons to the target, while keeping you safely defended.

I've come to believe that in a life and death situation, there is really no such thing as a "STYLE" for survival – it's a question of your own imagination – what the Buddhists refer to as your "fore-nature" – your "higher self," your innermost being – decides to do <u>at that moment,</u> to survive.

Nature equips each of us with our own set of senses to respond to that moment: You might wind up doing a move that you've learned, never used, and long since forgotten that you knew; or maybe even pull one out of your being that you'd never seen or heard of before, that fit the needs of that moment, to survive.

The art, correctly understood, teaches us to develop those senses by exploring movement, so that we can see and react without conscious recourse to thought, just as a kitten plays with its siblings to learn the skills it needs to know to survive. Ultimately, it's not what your sifu – your teacher – teaches you, that will save your life. It's about how you yourself APPLY that knowledge and training when you really need it.

We all tend to think our style, school, teacher, or system is "the best," but truthfully, I believe there is no one "best" style or system – there is only what you prefer: What you are loyal to, what you love best, what you believe in, what best suits your individual preferences and beliefs. Some people like the purity of a System, others just like what works for them.

It's like the old Zen story, which we Chinese call, "Chan" – it goes like this:

> A monk was once asked by his mother to go to the village butcher shop to buy meat for her dinner.

The monk is quite uncomfortable at this request, because monks aren't supposed to eat meat, but he was a dutiful son, and so, instead of telling her, "I can't! Monks aren't supposed to do that!" he does what his mother asks... But it's a real conflict for him.

So, feeling VERY self-conscious and embarrassed, into the shop he walks, very aware of all the looks he's getting from the people. And he compensates for his discomfort by saying in a loud voice, "GIVE ME THE BEST PIECE OF MEAT IN THE SHOP!"

"Every piece of meat in my shop is the best." the butcher answers with a friendly smile, "You cannot find one single piece of meat in my shop that is not the best!"

And at these words, the monk was enlightened.

So in that same sense, every "style" is the best, as the Chan masters say.

The martial arts are necessary. Self-defense is one of the first skills evolved by human beings. The world can be a dangerous place. Even the peaceful Buddhist monks had to have an effective way to defend themselves from bandits and wild beasts.

In the old days, these methods were taught to soldiers, or cultivated in monasteries, or existed in families, where they were passed on exclusively to family members or close friends, in strict secrecy.

Choy Li Fut happened to be a popular "style" in my region of China – and, eventually, it became the first of many, many, styles that I saw performed over the course of my life.

Originally it was not one style, but several styles: "Choy" was what we call a 'family style' of kung fu – a style that was once kept within a family – in this case the Choy Family, and taught only to family members, or close, proven friends. "Li" was another family style of kung fu – Actually, it's MY family name, too: Lee – "Lee" and "Li" are just different ways of writing the same character in English. And "Fut" was a Buddhist "long hand" system – an outfighting style of kung fu originally practiced by the monks.

Somewhere along the line, these three styles all combined to form the Choy Li Fut system in its present form.

But the first "style" that I actually trained in was the Shaolin style. You've probably seen the TV show, Kung Fu, where David Carradine plays Kwai Chang Caine, a wandering Shaolin monk, cast adrift in the American "Wild West" by circumstances beyond his control. In the series, Carradine's character was a Shaolin stylist – a monk trained at the famed Shaolin Temple in Henan Provence.

Not many people know this, but the show was actually Bruce Lee's idea. He wanted to play the part of "Caine," but at the time, Hollywood didn't believe that a Chinese actor in a leading role would be accepted by American audiences.

At the time, Bruce was known for the role of "Kato;" the part he played on "The Green Hornet" TV series. That was OK, of course: It wasn't a lead role, and the idea that Newspaper Publisher Brit Reed – who was secretly the "Green Hornet" – had a trusted Chinese sidekick, had been around ever since the first debut of the radio show, back in 1936... It contributed to the mysterious and exotic appeal of the "Green Hornet" character. So Bruce had that screen credit – the studios knew he was talented and could act.

And of course there were other precedents for minorities being cast as sidekicks for TV's iconic "masked avengers" – the Lone Ranger's close friend and faithful sidekick, Tonto, was another iconic example of that tested, proven formula...

Eric, Kailani & Jason Lee

But TV series cost a lot of money to make, and Hollywood was nervous about casting an Asian-American in the lead role: Ultimately, he didn't get the part, but he did eventually prove them all wrong. Audiences were more accepting than the Hollywood of that time thought they would be.

Today we watch Asian actors like Jackie Chan, Jet Li, Donnie Yen, Lucy Liu, or Michelle Yeoh, in lead roles without a second thought. But Bruce Lee's talent and ambition kicked those doors open, and he deserves credit for that.

People have commented more than once that my lifestyle really does resemble that of a modern Kwai Chang Caine:

I never really thought about it, but I suppose it does in a vague sort of way – I like travel and new adventures like the character in that series... Although I rarely wander around the desert - I usually get around by car, plane, or train, and I definitely prefer it that way. And I don't typically have encounters with violent cowboys... but I am a martial artist like "Caine;" and, like the character, I love to explore new places and meet new people.

I'm a "people person," like the character, "Caine," is – I really LIKE people. I always have. I find them fascinating. We all have different experiences in life, but the same mind, the same spirit as all human beings possess...I have friends from all walks of life – rich people, poor people, famous people, unknown people people of all cultures and colors and backgrounds... Everybody is the same to me. Different belief systems, different bodies, different color – who cares! Those are minor things.

I like to think I'm a "good guy" like the "Caine" character – but I suppose that just about everybody believes that – It's why we identify with "Caine," as a character, after all.

Like "Caine," I'm fortunate in that I have a lot of freedom to do what I want to do; so now that I think of it, maybe I am like him in a way...

But although I'm a martial artist and a grandmaster, I'm not a monk, like the character, "Caine" is. I think of myself mainly as an artist and a movie maker, although I do have a few other skills as well. I don't have to wander around the desert on foot – I do love to walk, and I walk several miles each day, but I have a car of my own, thankfully, and a house of my own, and I enjoy them. So I suppose you could say that I like my "creature comforts" a bit more than "Caine" does...

But by the same token, I live in a modest house, and I drive a very "ordinary" car, and tend to give away more than I accumulate. I see a lot of people who get caught up in the "rat race," and wind up

> "Eric Lee? How many people would walk off a movie set in L.A. and come clear to Thailand to watch over you when you're sick? Eric did.
>
> "I was doing two movies, 'Blood Sport II and Blood Sport III, in Thailand, and I got deathly sick... I actually went into a coma for 10 days...
>
> "When Eric found out about that, he literally dropped everything, and came to stay with me in the hospital until I recovered, AND flew me home when I got better.
>
> "He paid his OWN way back and forth from Thailand to be there with me... Then he came back to L.A. and finished the movie. That's Eric."
>
> -Nancy Chavez, Lima Lama black belt

struggling to pay for all the "stuff" they've got. It's as if all that property owns THEM, rather than the other way around. I don't want to be like that – I want to be free to go out and enjoy life.

So I'm not "owned" by my possessions, and I don't define my success in life by the things I have accumulated. Most people concentrate on what they DON'T have. But for the sake of my own health and happiness, I like to focus on what I DO have: I like that saying, "Count your blessings." It's true.

I like my freedom. I like exploring new places, and finding new things to learn and do.

Thankfully, unlike "Caine," I don't have to depend exclusively on myself and my kung fu skills: If I want to get something done, and it involves skills that I don't know, I delegate – I find somebody that DOES know that skill. That's a specialty of mine, and one that I've learned to be good at. I work with people who are experts, specialists with high-level skills, who know how to get it done. You have to!

Especially when putting together a movie – which is one of the things I love to do – it's necessary. Cameramen, lighting technicians, directors, writers, actors... each one of them brings skills that require decades of training to perfect. I don't have all those skills! Nobody does. Nobody can do it all, by themselves. So first, you find the people who have knowledge. Second, of those who have the knowledge, you find those who have the drive and experience to get the job done.

So I talk to people. That's key. My particular specialty lies in getting ideas for projects, finding the people I need, and putting it all together. Most people see only the pieces of the puzzle, without grasping the plan... But my job is to see the "Big Picture" and put everybody's work together, like a general that plans the battle. That's what I do.

But I digress.

As I've said, the first "style" that I studied was the Shaolin style. A friend of mine was kind enough to share his knowledge of that style with me. Later, I exchanged with another friend of mine named Patrick, and learned Southern Style Praying Mantis, and Drunken Mantis... and I also studied the Hung Gar form and some other Southern styles, during my time in Hong Kong. Naturally, the more you learn, the easier it becomes to pick up other styles.

When it came to kung fu, I was like a kid in a candy shop... I studied Chin-na, Dao In, and of course, the Northern Shaolin and Shaolin style; which was the most popular because of the fame of the monks; and also Five Elements style... and Buddhist style with a teacher named Chung Bal, and perhaps a few others... So many, really, that I can't keep track of them all, anymore. These days I do what *I* do. My "style" is just my own natural movement. I didn't intend to "create" it – it evolved all by itself.

Eventually, I "specialized" in Kajukenbo and Won Hop Kune Do under Sifu Al Dacascos, and I became well known as a practitioner of these systems. But I also studied Judo with Wally Jay, and "Judo Gene" LeBell; and Jun Fan Gung Fu and Bruce Lee's modified systems of kung fu and JKD with James Yimm Lee... and

I also studied the "AG Matrix System" which is a Lima Lama offshoot developed by Al Garza. I liked that system, because its methods provide ways of developing a whole lot of relaxed, natural power for a small guy like me… I studied so many different methods.

I also studied Chi Gung energy healing with Grandmaster Share K. Lew, and Tai Chi and Chi Gung with Master Wen Mei Yu… And I am also the designated successor of Dr. Hua Huang's Medical Chi Gung – he has passed on, so his skills are with me now… I'm now the caretaker of that knowledge.

So Chi Gung is also a specialty of mine, although it isn't widely known or practiced in the West.

I earned a 7th degree in Sifu Al Dacascos' Won Hop Kuen Do, and a 9th Degree in Kajukenbo, and I know more than 40 martial arts weapons. At 72, I can still do them all – even difficult, very physical ones like the 9-section chain whip.

When somebody asks me what my favorite weapon is, I can't resist joking a bit: I tell them "Oh! Rocket launcher with GPS system!" Well? I mean, if you had a choice, why not, right? :)

Today, Tai Chi is one of my most favorite things to do.

"Tai Chi" in Chinese means "grand ultimate" – but it can be interpreted in a variety of ways.

"Chi" for us Chinese is "life energy." It is said that you can live without food for about a month, and you can live without water for a few days, and you can even live without air for a few minutes, but you cannot live without chi for even one instant.

The chi flows when you are absolutely relaxed, and your mind is clear and free of thought. That's what Tai Chi is all about.

In Chinese thought, Chi is believed to be concentrated in the "tan tien" – a point about 3 inches below the navel, and it flows throughout the body on a regular timetable that is controlled by the human bio-clock. We believe that it governs health and well-being.

But in practical application – martial arts-wise – it is also said to be rooted in the feet, released through the legs, controlled by the

> "I met Eric after his martial arts career, so I know him as a friend. He's a very loyal friend, always helping whoever he can. He has a creative mind, he's a great organizer, He can put together an event and it all works out – Amazing! He's also an excellent musician. He picks up a new instrument and quickly becomes proficient. Recently, he's really gotten into doing his Tai Chi – He's good! He has his own style..."
>
> - Bob Whiteside, Tai Chi practitioner

waist, and made manifest in the hands – That's a famous Tai Chi saying, and it's a very good brief description of how it all works.

These days I can spend hours doing Tai Chi, being one with the motion, losing myself in the movement until I forget all sense of "I" and the MOVEMENT seems to do ME, and not the other way around: That's when the "chi" flows.

The complete relaxation and freedom of the mind from even itself, promotes healing and cultivation of what we call "intrinsic energy," or "life energy." For the martial arts it means vastly enhanced reactions, perfect timing, and power in the strike from perfect alignment and accuracy, – and for the body and the mind, it means more freedom from stress, enhanced health and longevity.

These are things that are just beginning to be understood and researched in the West, in much the same way that acupuncture was "discovered" by the West in the 1970s and found to be effective by western scientists.

There was the famous story about the western journalist who became ill with appendicitis while covering President Nixon's groundbreaking trip to China, and instead of using anesthetics, the doctors used acupuncture – he was perfectly conscious during the procedure, of course, and if memory serves, I believe the man was even given an orange to eat while the doctors were working on him. Well, as you can imagine, at the time, this was like magic in the West, and it generated enough interest and excitement that people here started to research it - and guess what? They found out that it works!

We knew that all along, of course. In China these are our traditional healing arts – acupuncture, herbs, Tai Chi, Chi Gung, all of that is part of our culture.

So that's what I'm doing now, martial arts-wise – that and the forms that are my favorites. That's how I keep my skills sharp today. As we get older, we cannot do the incredible physical things that we did in our 20s, but on the other hand, why would we?

The tradeoff between a young, strong martial artist and a mature, experienced martial artist, is that we discover new ways of moving more efficiently and economically, so that it is not NECESSARY to do all the extraordinary physical things that we did in our younger days; and conversely, even a young, strong, martial artist can run out of endurance at a key moment if he spends energy unwisely.

For a mature martial artist, the quest is one of "less is more" – getting better by doing less – meaning: "being efficient." The "right" reaction, contact at the right spot, at the right moment, with the right weapon, and the body in perfect position in relation to the opponent's.

As remarkable as those amazing physical feats of the martial arts are – backflips, acrobatics, and so forth – they also burn up a LOT of energy and endurance, that can be saved by employing more efficient movement: Eventually, as we get older and more skilled, we reach a place where we say to ourselves, "Why work that hard?"

Basically, "never spend a foot when an inch will suffice."

I was a skilled technician when I was a young man, which is good… A young man should have a good technical vocabulary, and I did: I could do all sorts of jumps and acrobatics… I had energy to burn. But I also have to say, I also wasted a LOT of energy. I feel that I move a LOT more efficiently as an older man, than I did when I was young.

Younger men have more endurance, strength, agility, and durability – that's true. It's also true that if you move "right," strength tends to be less of a factor. If you attack the right points, your opponent's "durability" ceases to be an issue… and if you move where the opponent isn't expecting you to be, and understand how to correctly anticipate his movements, then your own durability is less of a factor as well.

Real fights tend to only last for a few brief seconds – so vast levels of endurance are far less crucial than they are in a tournament where you must defeat a number of opponents, or a boxing match where you have to survive for 12 long, grueling rounds.

But these are really just things with which we occupy our minds with in training. Truthfully, after more than half a century of daily practice to keep the skills "sharp," the body is trained to react automatically, as naturally as a striking snake, the spirit naturally seeks peaceful outcomes, and the chi flows in a natural way, like an endless river.

In combat, of course, the body has its OWN mind and it instinctively knows how to react – so the saying goes that "I" don't hit – "IT" hits: That is true.

So continuing to research newer, more efficient ways of moving, and polishing our technique is merely an intellectual pursuit, a way of staying fit, and an interesting and enjoyable way to pass our time constructively and add to our understanding of the martial arts –

I still love to do that, of course. What can I say I was always a fanatic about training. When I was a young man, I wanted to learn anything and everything anybody had to teach. I learned empty hand kung fu skills, and also learned weapons, which became a sort of specialty of mine – we treat the weapon as an extension of your own arm. I know the sets to 40 different Chinese weapons, and I am at the point where I can move all these weapons as naturally and spontaneously as I would move my own hands.

Not many people know the sword anymore. At one time it was an indispensable part of a man's knowledge. In these days we have things like guns, but in the old days, things like swords and spears, and arrows were important. They were the way that armies fought and the way that people protected themselves and their loved ones before there were guns or a police force, or 911.

Believe me, something like a sword can really get in the way if you're not used to living with it as a natural part of your own body, so that moving around with it becomes second-nature. Otherwise, it's kind of like the old slapstick comedy routines where the guy is walking around while carrying a long two-by-four on his shoulder, knocking people down left and right. Worse, because it's sharp.

Fighting with a sword isn't just a matter of clashing the blades edge-to-edge as you often see in the movies – unavoidable as that may be in the heat of the moment, contact like that can nick a fine blade, damaging it, or even breaking it. You can see this in antique swords that have been through desperate battles, and you think to yourself, "if only it could talk…"

But damage like that wasn't by design. A sword with a notched, chipped, or damaged blade is a story, written in steel: It's a record, an indication that its owner made a mistake, or perhaps didn't have time to parry an unexpected move properly. In the old days swords were precious – they were a lifeline for their owners, and so they did all they could do to keep them intact and undamaged.

Even those dull movie swords can be quite dangerous if you're not careful. For example, if a blade gets nicked while filming a fight scene, that sharp nick can cut you just as surely as a razor-honed edge, and in any event, the sword's point is sharp enough to do real damage if the slightest mistake is made. So even stunt players using dull swords have to REALLY know what they are doing to make the scene look real while protecting themselves and each other.

Ask any actor who has filmed scenes with swords – great care has to be taken to work-up each sequence until it becomes second-nature, in order to minimize injuries, and even then you get dings and bruises. It just comes with the territory.

On the set, you have to know how to DEFLECT the enemy's sword with the back or the flat of the blade – That part of the blade is used for "blocking," while preserving the edge from developing those dangerous, sharp little nicks. And of course, it's the same in combat: You have to use the strong parts of the sword to parry and deflect, and preserve the edge for cutting the enemy.

If a man who really knows how to move a blade, I can see it instantly. I can tell the difference between a man who is skilled with a stick or a dull blade, and a man who has worked extensively with a real sword and has a "sense of the edge." You can see it in the movement of someone who really knows how to cut with a sword. No disrespect intended! The stick can be just as deadly as a sword – It's just that the skills are not the same: The movement is subtly "different," and that difference is unmistakable. You can SEE it in the motion.

A real swordsman is aware of the edge at every instant. He HAS to be. With only an instant of carelessness, your own blade can cut you just as deeply as a skilled opponent's – You're essentially moving a 3-foot razor all around you, and you have to be aware of that at all times. That unwavering, constant, continuous awareness is your only protection, and you have to practice it *until it becomes a part of you* – second nature. And similarly, even a razor-sharp sword will not reliably cut well without a practiced, intuitive understanding of the technique involved. Swords aren't built for chopping like an axe – rather, the edge is either retracting or extending as it hits, slicing as well as hitting, to maximize its cutting power – that's how a sword really cuts. Even a fine sword with a razor-sharp blade will not cut well without correct technique.

That's a subtle skill, but a REAL skill, a CRUCIAL skill for a real swordsman. There are many people who can zip through a kata with a dull practice sword, and look *spectacular* – jumping, spinning, slinging the sword around effortlessly, as hard as they can... They look fantastic... You go, "Wow! Looks GREAT!"

...But typically, you can watch their eyes "get big" if you hand them a real, razor-sharp sword and say, "Here. Try it with this." A good sword can shave the hair from an arm as cleanly as any razor: The instant you pick up one of those, and realize exactly what you're handling, and what it can do to a human body with only one tiny mistake, the whole picture changes.

And in all fairness, sure, in tournament competition it makes solid sense to err on the side of caution and use a practice sword, just for the sake of others' safety, if not your own –

My only point is that the use of a real sword is a completely different game, a different skill, requiring a whole new level of awareness: The difference is like night-and-day.

In the course of my training, I learned "short weapons" – swords, and sword and shield – "long weapons" like staff, and spear... And I learned the kwan do – a pole arm: the big, broad-bladed chopping weapon that you see in the Chinese movies. I even learned exotic weapons like three-section staff, and Nine-section chain whip and sword – skills that are rare even in China...

In addition to weapons, like many Asian martial artists I learned some of the more exotic systems of energy healing, like Reiki and Chi Gung energy healing... My Chi Gung teacher, Dr. Hua Huang, made the point that if I learned how to kill, I also had to learn how to heal... I became his successor when he passed on, so I now carry his knowledge inside me.

While I am perhaps best known for my Kajukenbo and Won Hop Kune Do, I am "eclectic" in that sense. But more accurately, after so many years of training my motion is my own, now, not a product of any fixed "style" or external or artificial way of moving – I've become one with the motion, now – I've forgotten "this style and "that style" - It's just how I move. "Style" is just a tool to use until your body learns the secrets of how to move itself.

You could say that Chinese opera, and my father's Choy Li Fut style, and the old kung fu movies I saw in Hong Kong –were my first images of the art. I wasn't a martial artist then – I didn't really begin my training until I was 13 or 14 – in those days I played soccer! I suppose that's how I first got my physical endurance, as a child. I always had a lot of energy, and soccer gave me an outlet... But those images were implanted in my memory, in my being. At the time, of course, I had no idea that they would shape my life as they did, but looking back, that is where it all began:

Life is like that.

Eric's Sibling

Gerald Okamura & Eric Lee on Weapons of Death Set

(Kung-fu)

"It is not because things are difficult that we do not dare; it is because we do not dare that they are difficult." – Seneca

CHAPTER THREE: Exploring the Martial Arts...

— "YOU don't hit: IT hits." — Martial arts saying

When I was a young man, the path I discovered was martial arts. The martial arts are a philosophical "Way," like Zen — which we Chinese call "Chan" — They are not discovered by the mind's cleverness, or artificial contrivances, but by the very nature of the art, and the constant practice of it. Their essence cannot be confined to a fixed curriculum or lesson plan: It is a living art that must be experienced, taken-in, and understood intuitively through hard work, deep thought, and constant practice:

Eventually it "speaks" to you in a way, and it becomes a living part of you. It's one of those arts where the whole is greater than the sum of all the parts — that may seem self-contradictory, but it's true.

The "philosophy" of kung fu is also "taught," true, but it is mainly discovered WITHIN by direct insight — those insights have been

Chuck Norris in middle

carefully understood and passed down from teacher to student, from the beginning:

As the student gains skill and becomes a practitioner, and eventually, a master, such insights are gained and passed on to a new generation.

The martial arts are about far more than fighting. Actually, I believe that the fighting skill is actually only a very small part of what the Art is about. Martial arts are a comprehensive lifestyle, a way of life.

Today, martial artists tend to emphasize physical skills, much like boxing, or wrestling, or professional sports. But true martial arts is not a sport. It is different: quite separate and distinct. Why? *Because to have professional sports, you have to have <u>survivors</u>.*

When I began my training in the art, fighting was for real. It was serious. It was life and death. That was the emphasis, the purpose – it was not about winning, or about sports – it was about surviving a life-and-death encounter with an opponent – or opponents – who were determined to kill you, handed down from a time before guns made such skills secondary. The mindset

> "Eric Lee is a great participant, a great teacher, and a great human being... And tougher than John Wayne! ...But he's not handsome like me!"
>
> -"Judo Gene" LeBell – judo and jujitsu expert, master grappler and wrestler, boxer, veteran Hollywood stuntman, author, and martial arts legend.

is completely different. Paradoxically, that mindset makes you more inclined to peace – rational people naturally want to avoid encounters like that.

In ancient times, before guns, tanks, and mechanized warfare evolved, combat was done by at close quarters, hand-to-hand – usually with weapons, but sometimes without. Battles were engaged in by warriors who underwent intense training and conditioning, and they had to have both mental and physical preparation – not only just to improve their odds at survival and to win battles, but also to cope with the tremendous mental and emotional stress of facing the prospect of battle under those conditions.

When you stop and think about those times, it becomes easier to understand how the attitudes and philosophies of martial arts evolved.

If you were a warrior in those days, even if it was peaceful all around you at that moment, the anticipation of battle under such savage conditions must have generated incredible levels of stress. You had to be properly prepared both mentally and physically... and also spiritually, in order to be able to accept that reality and live day-to-day life without being burdened by it.

Over the centuries, certain proven attitudes and practices emerged and were naturally handed down from one generation to the next.

THAT is where the philosophy of the martial arts evolved. That is how it all came about – The training, meditation, and ways of strong, quiet thought gave warriors the means to relax, to let go of killer levels of stress and live their lives normally; until the actual moment came that they had to face those hardships of life in the field, and the terrors of battling men with swords, spears, and arrows.

Modern-day competition can be tough, of course, but next to that reality, even the roughest tournament about pales in comparison. Sure, you might get bruised up in competition, or even have bones broken or other injuries. But in sports, you have every reason to believe that you probably won't die in the ring… that you and your opponent will be around the next day – otherwise, why would you do it?   Hopefully, you'd be smart enough to find something else to do for a living – Dying isn't much of a living.

Our ancestors in the martial arts often didn't have the luxury of that choice. Thankfully, today we do. But the trade-off is that we may not train with quite the same deadly serious intent.

Meaning absolutely no disrespect to the courage, skill, and physical conditioning of modern fighters – all of which I respect… but even the way the fighters are TAUGHT makes it less likely that they or their opponent will die in the ring.

People think that full contact fighting which we see today is "all out" – and it IS, in a sense… But the reality is that there are still rules. And the simple truth is that the rules are there to help keep the fighters ALIVE, and help safeguard them from the prospect of permanent, serious injuries. It HAS to be that way: If fighters consistently died in the ring or soon thereafter, the sport would quickly be banned.

If the existing rules were actually researched exhaustively and fighters modified their training in ways that were designed to exploit those rules to the fullest extent possible, there would be many more deaths and serious injuries. Thankfully, at least so far, nobody wants that. We want to protect life and guard against serious injuries in our sporting events. That's why boxers wear gloves, and martial artists like Jigoro Kano created the sport of judo modified Jiu Jitsu by taking out the more lethal moves, so that competitions could be held in relative safety.

Our humanity has evolved past the days of the Gladiators in the Roman Coliseum. Today it is considered reprehensible to kill for sport and for the gratification of the crowd, and hopefully it will STAY that way.

But by the same token, the TRUE martial arts are not about sport, or winning a competition or taking home money, or a trophy – They are about *survival* – skills to protect your village, your family, your loved ones... yourself. Those were hard truths that people actually had to live with in ancient times.

Not surprisingly many of the styles that evolved in families or schools were highly secret, because if a rival clan or army learned what techniques and methods you were using, counters could be devised that could cost lives.

So the true Art is very different from the sport. The EMPHASIS is simply on a different result. In ancient times, those life and death insights were regarded as real treasures, and that wisdom was carefully preserved and handed down from one generation to the next. That is the martial arts.

The world has changed a great deal since those arts evolved. And yet, in some ways, it hasn't.

Unfortunately, I personally learned the importance of this lesson the hard way, on the mean streets of Oakland, California, as a boy, after I had moved to America. Oakland has a reputation as a "dangerous place," and from my own experience, there's some truth to that.

Someone I was with at the time, a big kid – and to this day, I don't know who he was or why he did this – but he said, "Hey, Eric! Look up at that!"

Well, I looked up. And that was a big mistake: Without warning he chopped me hard across the throat. He probably intended it as some sort of cruel joke, and had no idea what could happen.

But the blow hit me across my windpipe, and must have also struck the vagus nerve, the nerve in the neck that controls the heart and the lungs:

Well, I "went out," I was completely unconscious. When I came to, I lay there for literally hours, unable to move, struggling to breathe. Gradually, I came back to life. But I could easily have died that day… So far as I know, it was done for no reason whatsoever – just because of another human being's stupidity and lack of humanity.

I never saw that person again. I don't know his name, I don't remember what he looked like – other than that he was huge – it was so many years ago, he's probably dead by now... But when I was young, it was different.

As I'm sure you can imagine, that experience made me deeply angry. I plunged HARD into my training with revenge in my heart. I wanted to find my attacker and make him pay. I wanted to hurt the guy, as he had hurt me...

But somewhere along the way, that negative experience became unimportant... I no longer had to carry it inside. I was able to put it down and understand that this intense, white-hot anger harmed nobody but me. I learned to forget, and ultimately to forgive. I learned to appreciate the beauty of the art, and the experience of discovering, learning, understanding. The discovery of The Way of the martial arts.

So today, I want to thank that guy, because that chop on the throat gave me the motivation to learn and to train hard, to approach training with deadly serious intent, and immerse myself in the art.

Thankfully, a violent encounter like mine isn't a necessary requisite for finding your personal path, though... It can be anything. It can be the sound of a particular musical instrument, or the sun on your face and the scent of the grass on a long, perfect summer day... Literally anything might be the "switch" that turns on that inner desire.

Before discovering The Way of your life's path, comes the desire, the vision, the fire within – the Inner Voice that says, "YES! THAT is what I need! That is what I want to do." And that IS what you need: That inner fire, that true desire to learn, is the real requirement for learning and mastering the art.

There's an old story: I don't remember where I first heard it, I wish I did. I think it was related to me as a story from famed JKD instructor and Kali guro Dan Inosanto...

...But the story goes that a student once came to the home of an old master...

> The old master lived in the village, and since he was very familiar with all the families there, he knew that this particular young man, at that stage in his life, was very frivolous and flighty - he did not have the makings of a serious student – he was always flitting from one interest to another; trying new things – but instead of settling down and doing the work of learning, he would discover some new fascination in a few days, and that would be that. So he had a well-known reputation for wasting his own time, and the time of those who tried to teach him.
>
> So when the young man appeared at the master's door, saying "Sifu, teach me the martial arts," the master Immediately grabbed the student and dragged him to a fast-running stream that flowed behind his house, and he forced the student's head underwater.

After a long time, he pulled the student up, sputtering and gasping for air.

"WHAT DID YOU FEEL?" The master demanded.

"Teacher," said the confused and traumatized student truthfully, "I felt an intense desire to breathe!"

"Come back when you feel exactly that way about learning the martial arts," the master said.

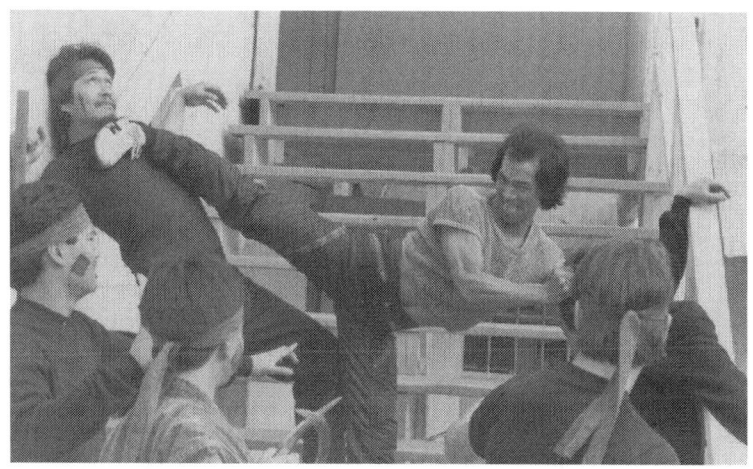

(Harmony)

"Be really whole and all things will come to you."

– Lao Tzu

CHAPTER FOUR: Life in my Village

"Back then, life was very different!"

As I've said, I was born in Fu Chung Village in Canton, China, a little village of only about 125 people. I was born on July 30, 1946, just before sunrise. That's the "Year of the Dog" according to the traditional Chinese zodiac, and according to the Western zodiac, I'm a "Leo," according to my birth-month.

I feel I should say a few words about Fu Chung, so that I can share with you a sense of my origin, and perhaps, some feeling for what life was like in those days.

Fu Chung Village was typically quiet, and very simple back then. Thankfully, the soldiers I told you about came only once, and ordinarily, life was quite peaceful, except for the hurricanes that visited on occasion. Those storms were bad – lots of lightning, wind, and rain – but they were a natural part of life, too.

Like all the people in the village, I was a natural born baby – there were no hospitals and no shots in those days… no Western-trained doctors. When my time came to be born, my mother cut my umbilical cord with a pair of scissors.

I was 6 years old before I saw my first canned food. All the food in Fu Chung Village was strictly organic food only – there was no canned food. I never even saw cans or knew that canned food even existed until we moved to Hong Kong.

When we got sick or injured, we used herbs to treat these conditions. That was what we used back then, and each family had its own medicines and home remedies.

That's life. Life is connected to the land itself, and the people are a natural product of that connection. We all literally belong to the land, and whether we realize it or not, we still live our whole lives connected to it – it still gives us the food we eat and the water we drink. And when we die, we return to the land. It's easy to lose touch with that truth in a modern world, but this is true for all people everywhere, whether we realize it or not.

Today, we're all used to pills and capsules, and so herbal remedies may seem a bit "exotic" to some... But all medicines originally came from plants and minerals, and if you visit Chinatown in major cities like Los Angeles or San Francisco, you can see the traditional herb shops that still dot the streets, and provide us with medicines for health and healing. I have an intimate connection with places like this –they're like home to me...

It's a puzzle when you think about it: How did we learn, as human beings, that one plant was good to heal wounds, or another plant was good for pain, or fever? That knowledge was handed down to us, from healers who communed with nature and got their wisdom from direct experience, and passed their knowledge along to the next generation... and the next... and the next after that, down through the ages.

So the earth has a lot of wisdom for us, if we stay close to it and learn to "listen."

That truth was easy to understand in Fu Chung. I think it's much harder for kids born to cities, and supermarkets, and video games to grasp.

So you can see how much life has changed for us.

I have a little insight into that, because I was able to experience that transition from village to city first hand, first when our family moved to Hong Kong, and later when I came to America.

I was always an active child, running around a lot to burn up energy... I still have all that energy, which is a mixed blessing: Sometimes I have a hard time chasing all the thoughts out of my head so that I can relax... But on the other hand, today at 72, I can still do everything that I always did, so I suppose it's a good trade-off.

I still eat a lot – about the only foods I don't love are salty foods, fried foods, or dairy products, and I have no real taste for sweets... So I guess I'm lucky in that way. I naturally 'eat healthy.'

I'm still very active and I still wear out my little Jack Russell terrier, Bela, on our walks. In today's world I might be labeled hyperactive, but thankfully, in those days we were allowed to just be ourselves, and I was spared all that negativity. If I was "hyperactive" it has served me pretty well in life. Actually, I don't take Bela for a walk – she takes ME for a walk!   But when she gets tired, she lies down and won't move, and I wind up having to carry her. That's not bad for 72.

When I was very young, I was REALLY active. I spent my early days playing with my two cousins, fishing and catching catfish, climbing fruit trees and eating apples, lychee nuts, oranges, bananas, and longan fruit. I had a huge appetite. I still do. A tricycle was my only toy.

We had a well that we drew water from, and there were frogs that lived there. Sometimes I would try to catch them, or just spend time watching them swim and move, and live their very different lives.

My father, my mother, my sisters, and even my great-grandparents on my father's side lived in the house. One custom that Westerners may find odd was that it was sometimes the custom to buy a coffin before death, and my great grandmother did that. Believe it or not, it sat behind the front door of our house. I always left it alone - It *bothered* me. I NEVER played around it... She bought it when she was in her 80s, but she didn't die until she was 104.

When Grandmother finally passed away, many people came to pay their respects – In China, the belief is that old age is good luck, so people will come to pay their respects to a very old person who has passed on. Part of the custom for her passing was that I had to carry water from the river and bring it back home. I was very young when this happened of course, and I– to this day I don't know the customs and traditions behind it.

The Chinese custom, like the American custom, is that funerals are sad. Actually, I like the Hawaiian funeral customs better, because for them, a funeral is a celebration of life. The people get together and celebrate the life of the person – they hold a big luau to send the one who has passed away, off in style. I think that's a more positive custom.

When there was a wedding – both sides of family would bring whatever food they had – pigs, chickens, whatever was at hand – they would exchange food to celebrate, and we would cook it in a huge wok.

I still have some of my family's heirlooms from those old days – I have my grandparents' traditional clay wedding pillows, and mom's wedding robe from Cheng Dynasty, which was the last great imperial dynasty of China – you could call these things "family treasures" – I certainly treasure them. They're like a piece of my heritage…

I enjoy my cars and my home, and my American name, and English language, and all the comforts that life in a modern society provides, but I still have these things to remind me of where I came from.

Each year we had the Moon Festival... The Moon Festival is a harvest festival that occurs on the 15th day of the eighth lunar month – August 15th.

According to the legend surrounding it, a great hero named Hou Yi lived during a time when 10 scorching-hot suns came to fill the sky overhead. The heat became so intense that the people were dying. So Hou Yi shot down nine of the suns, with his bow and arrows (Those must have been SOME bows and arrows!) and he saved the people.

Legend has it that as a reward he was given a magic potion by the Queen of Heaven, which would make him immortal and cause him to mingle with the stars and fly away to the moon. But Hou Yi didn't drink the potion, because he loved his wife, Chung Err, and wanted to stay with her forever. So he gave her the potion and told her to watch over it, as a gesture of his true love for her. He loved her so much that he was willing to reject immortality itself to spend the rest of his life with her.

Here the plot thickens: One of Hou Yi's students was a sneaky, dishonest fellow who conspired to steal the potion from her, drink it, and become immortal himself. But Chung Err; who was the essence of a dutiful wife, and absolutely loyal to her husband's wishes that she was to guard the potion; came across the student before he could accomplish his evil plans. In the ensuing struggle, she was forced to take the drastic measure of drinking the potion herself, to keep him from it.

Sadly, just as foretold by the Queen of Heaven, she instantly became immortal, flying away to the moon. And ever since, the loyal Hou Yi has always looked for his lost love.

So this tale, is a sort of romantic festival for us: After all, the legend is about true love - two people who are deeply in love with each other, who have been separated by circumstances beyond their control. Special, sweet, traditional "moon cakes" are made and eaten as the moon rises.

It's a family event – the family gathers and spends the day together. Lovers meet each other at the festival, or, if somehow, circumstances prevent them from being together, they go outside and look at the moon – each knowing that the other is also looking up in wonder at the same moon, and thinking of them.

The people pray to Chung Err for good fortune, and sing "moon poems." It is said that when the moon rises high in the sky, if you look really hard, you can see Chung Err dancing on the moon, waiting faithfully for Hou Yi to return to her at long last.

And of course, we also had our Chinese New Year, which we all celebrate. We had firecrackers for fun. They were popular for celebrations especially at New Year. We also had "lucky money" at New Year, in fancy, red envelopes, called "Lai see" – the red color is a symbol of energy, happiness, and good luck, so sending red envelopes is a way to send good wishes and good fortune – it's believed to bestow happiness and blessings on the person you give it to, and it's considered impolite to open it in front of the giver.

Perhaps you've seen Bruce Lee's "Return of the Dragon" where he's given a red envelope containing money – We did that.

Of course, the world is far different today. This was before men had walked on the moon, before everyone had computers, or cell phones, or cars, or television, or video games.

So that was life in Fu Chung Village. It was much simpler back then which must be hard for today's generation to imagine.

Eric Lee's Great Grandfather

Eric Lee's Great Grandmother

She lived to be 104 years old.

(Brave)

"In the middle of every difficulty lies opportunity." – Albert Einstein

CHAPTER FIVE: We Move to Hong Kong

"Wow! This is a REALLY big village!"

In 1952, when I was 6 years old, my family moved to the Kowloon district of Hong Kong, where my father planned to open an herb shop. I told you that Herb shops were like home to me, remember? Now you know why.

My father, Shao Nam Lee, was a serious man, always very strict and frugal. For example, I was such an active child, I used to wear out a lot of shoes, so dad made me super-tough "tire sandals," that NEVER wore out – I'm active, but even I don't put the mileage on like a car does, so that worked out well. Father was very thrifty - tight with a dollar – and so he did well in business.

He was also great at photography and electronics which he did as a hobby. He was really good! He actually made transistor radios that we listened to. This absolutely fascinated me as a child – I wondered how the people got into such a tiny space to speak.

Father liked Hong Kong, and this was a big, well-thought-out step for him. All Chinese people have at least some herbal knowledge – it's rather like Americans and Mickey Mouse, we are literally born to it. But my father was quite knowledgeable about herbs, and so, funded by my grandfather, we moved to Hong Kong, to open up an herb shop.

I was very excited at my first glimpse of Hong Kong – it was a brand new world for me, with shops, streets, and bicycles. I said to myself, "Wow! This village is so BIG!" I had no idea HOW big.

Even back then, Hong Kong was a huge city. As you can imagine, coming from a little village of 125 people, I had never seen anything like it!

Later, when we became well-established, my family lived upstairs in our herb shop, but when we first came to Hong Kong, we all lived in a house on the 2nd floor for three or four years.

My two sisters and I, my dad, and my grandmother, lived there, along with the high-level Chinese doctor who saw the patients, and our chef, who prepared the medicinal herbs for the customers, and also cooked for our family.

Our living area was on the 2th floor. We had to go downstairs for water, because the pump would not pump water up to the top level. But we did have street vendors who sold things like dried fruit, including one fellow who had – I guess you could call it a Chinese xylophone - that he used to attract customers and tell them that he was in the area. And this fellow would throw his wares – dried fruit, usually olives, wrapped in paper – up to us. He was amazing! He never missed! He threw the fruit upstairs, as easy as you please, and we would throw the money down to him – which of course was a lot easier.

There was another fellow, a street entertainer, who came by on a bicycle, with a HUGE jar of ginseng roots balanced on his head. Looking back on it, it seems odd, but people did these kinds of things for money – and it worked! We gave him money to go away!

Today I look back on all this as a unique part of my life, but back then I just accepted it without a second thought. That was just the way things were.

I also had a dog back then, a mixed German Shepherd named Lucky – that's "Ho Choy" in Cantonese. That dog and I were close. I was born the year of the dog, as I've told you – so perhaps that's why or maybe it's just that kids love dogs, and dogs love them back. There's a special bond that exists.

I still love dogs – Dogs are loyal, they love you no matter what – all they ask for is love, food, and play... Ho Choy and I were great playmates. One day we even fought and killed a rat who had invaded our territory. It was an adventure for both me and the dog.

Eventually, the family business expanded to two Herb shops, with two herbalists, and one actual, high-level Chinese doctor who read the pulses and prescribe formulas for his patients, and a chef who was responsible for cooking the fresh herbs correctly. We would buy them from dealers who would come by regularly. We were quite the entrepreneurial one family.

Hong Kong in those days was a British Crown Colony. It was even visited by Queen Elizabeth II once, when I was about 10. She's 92 now, but I remember her as a beautiful young woman – to me, she's still beautiful - she's the queen!

I liked living in Hong Kong. It was filled with excitement – always something to do! We could ride on the ferry, and there was lots of great food – Hong Kong had quite a "foodie" culture, and we often went out after midnight – the city never seemed to sleep! There was always lights and open shops and activity. I ventured out alone in the daytime, and I felt safe. I would usually go out with friends or my grandmother at night. We even have a word for it: "mon gai" - walking out on the street.

Hong Kong for me was like one giant carnival. It was a bustling, vibrant city, simply bristling with energy and excitement. There was lots of western music. At the time Elvis was very popular – we called him "the Cat," because of his strange, unique movements and gyrations. Ricky Nelson and Paul Anka were hot also. The place was booming until like 3 or 4 O'clock in the morning. It was fun! Like going to a huge, never-ending party. There were shops of all kinds and things to buy... And in those days, it was cheap! Quite affordable!

Everything was new to me. It really was like one big, giant carnival every night.

My favorite sport then was still soccer – we called it "football," of course. I played a lot, learned about herbs from constantly being around them in the herb shop, and watched a lot of black & white Kung Fu movies at the local theaters whenever I had money – admission was very cheap, and actually there were Western movies too.

There were LOTS of theaters in Hong Kong. We Chinese love our movies, just as Americans do. My uncle owned one that mainly showed – believe it or not – a lot of John Wayne movies; and there were many movies about the Chinese heroes and Shaolin monks, as well...

One night my grandmother found me sleepwalking – in route to the theater in my pajamas – it's the only time in my life I ever did sleepwalking. I must have been really eager to see that movie I was dreaming about, whatever it was.

I would watch Shih Kien – who later would play the evil villain "Mr. Han," in Bruce Lee's "Enter the Dragon..." I met him, years later, which was a great treat. He would often costar with another famous Hong Kong actor, Kwan Duk Ping, who played the famous Chinese Hung Gar (Tiger & Crane style) champion, Wong Fei Hung.

In America, when you think of "kung fu" you probably think instantly of Bruce Lee or Jackie Chan. But in China, when we think of kung fu, we think of Wong Fei Hung – he's the "Bruce Lee of China," although Bruce is now very famous in China, too.

Wong Fei Hung was a great master of the Hung Gar style, and an expert with the staff and the Southern tiger fork – which is a weapon that looks something like a pitchfork, with three sharp-pointed blades.

It really is a TIGER fork – it was originally made like that so that if you had to use one on a tiger, he couldn't run right up the spear's shaft, in spite of his wound, and kill you – whereas, if you used an ordinary spear, you'd be a goner. Even a clean, straight thrust right to the heart might not be enough to stop his charge until it was too late: Tigers can be fierce, that way.

I was fascinated by these early film martial artists, and the stories of the heroes they depicted. They were my "role models". Years later I learned the Hung Gar (Tiger and Crane) form, that Wong Fei Hung made famous, and I still do that form today, during demonstrations. So yes, they were definitely an influence.

One of the Chinese martial arts schools you may well have heard of, that I didn't get a chance to experience for myself, was the Chen Wu Association. If you've ever seen Bruce Lee in "The Chinese Connection" – the movie where he avenges a beloved teacher who has been poisoned by the bad guys – that's the Chen Wu Association. They're a real school, and their founder, Ho Yuan Cha, was a real master, and a famous one.

Most of the basic story behind that plot is real – he did fight and defeat foreign champions, and he is suspected to have been poisoned. Most Chinese know this story, it's part of our culture. That association was still in Hong Kong at that time, but I didn't train with them. I suppose I was too young, and wasn't ready... but the idea of becoming a real martial artist was already floating around in the back of my head.

One time I decided to explore some of these arts, though: I heard a rumor that some masters were going to get together for "high level" chi gung breathing – Really secret high level stuff!

So I figured "Wow, that sounds REALLY GREAT!!! This is my big chance! I've gotta see it!" - I planned to observe things, maybe pick up a little of that secret knowledge for myself...

But it turned out to be bad information: They were all doing "breathing exercises" all right! Whoever these guys were, all of them were sitting around smoking cigarettes by the carton! Ugh! The whole place was totally polluted with tobacco smoke! What a disappointment! So that joke was on me. Breathing exercises, right! Somebody undoubtedly had a good laugh over that one.

One real opportunity that did come my way was that one of the stars in those early movies was an actor named Lum Gau, and I was able to interact with him a bit. He was a friend of my father, and so I actually got to meet him. It was a great treat for me.

He told me a story about those early days of movies - They were doing a scene on the third floor of the set because in those days the cameras were very expensive and too heavy to move easily. So the actors had to shoot their fight scenes right up there on the third floor.

Shooting fight scenes – live action sequences – under those rudimentary conditions was VERY dangerous, and sure enough, Lum Gau fell: Three floors, straight down.

Maybe those floors weren't as high as the ones in the U.S. – I don't know, but it was still a long way down, especially if you're not expecting it. Somehow, though – with all that training, and the fear and adrenaline pumping through him from the fall, I suppose – Lum Gau landed in a perfect horse stance, BOOM, with no injury. Not a broken bone or a pulled muscle - not even a scratch. I wish they have that on film, it would have been an incredible stunt. That's real kung fu – real TESTED skill! But I'm sure he was happy just to be alive and unhurt.

Those stuntmen and actors in those Hong Kong movies have my respect: It's a tough way to make a living! For example, they didn't have break-away sugar "glass" in Hong Kong, like they do in Hollywood: If the script called for a stuntman to jump through a picture window, they simply found someone with the courage and skill to jump through REAL glass – Can you imagine? As I said, it's a tough way to make a living.

They had their own techniques for special effects, too… If they wanted to create the image of a supernaturally powerful punch, they'd use baby powder on the hand, so that it'd look like a puff of smoke. That strange, flapping sound effect that you always hear, when you see the actors flying on the screen? It is done by flapping a coat in the microphone.

Those fantastic, supernatural flying and jumping sequences that you always see in the Chinese movies? They were done by having the actors really jump DOWN from wherever they were filming and reversing the action in the lab.

Thankfully, they now use wires for flying sequences in movies like "The Matrix," or "Charlie's Angels," which is a lot safer for the actors – but in the old days they really did those things the hard way, and they had to have a lot of strength, skill, and toughness – and some luck, too – to survive.

If you can believe it, the big Hong Kong movie makers were always VERY secretive about the new movies they were working on, because they were afraid someone – some other movie maker – was going to steal their idea. They were SO secretive that there was no script! The director would tell you, "Ok, you're gonna say '1, 2, 3, 4, 5, 6, 7, 8, 9, 10!' - WITH EMOTION!" - And they would do voice-overs for those images, adding the words in after the filming was completed! Strange but true! Go figure people…

Actually, I still get a big kick out of seeing the differences between the Chinese and English versions of movies, because the closed captions aren't making an exact translation between the two languages – or if they're dubbed in English, they're trying to fit English words with the motions that the actors' mouths are making - and if you speak both languages, sometimes the differences are pretty funny.

I had a number of opportunities to make movies in Hong Kong, myself, but I always turned them down. The organized gangs in Hong Kong, the shadowy "Triads," as they are known, always wanted their "cut" of the profits – they're like the "Mob" here, organized crime – a widespread, tightly-knit secret society; very powerful, and very violent and dangerous if they are crossed. So between that and the expenses of the trip itself, you'd actually lose money to go.

I much preferred movies shot in America, with all the protections and residuals from the SAG/AFTRA union. We actors have it a lot better here, and I'm grateful to them for that. Thankfully, because I was just a kid in Hong Kong, and not an actor, I never had to contend with all of the perils and hardships that those Hong Kong actors faced.

I really enjoyed Hong Kong when I was there. Hong Kong is a port city and I went swimming and fishing in the ocean... And we visited Macao a couple times – They had wonderful seafood there, great crab and shrimp. And of course, we enjoyed the usual pastimes which are an integral part of our culture – We Chinese like to eat, make money, get together and talk.

Of course, I went to British schools in Hong Kong. It was the place I learned my first English. British teachers were strict, they would use a ruler to smash our hands for misbehavior, and I naturally resented that.

They weren't all strict, though: I was always a pretty good artist – I still paint and do Chinese calligraphy – and one time, when I was about 14, I was caught by the teacher, drawing a picture of a beautiful nude lady... It must have been a pretty good picture, because the teacher didn't punish me. In fact, he even asked if he could keep it for himself: What could I say but yes?

I became a "bad kid," because I used to cut classes and cook yams, and play with matches, which was foolish. I managed to set some things on fire that I shouldn't have, before I learned better.

Hong Kong was amazing during Chinese New Year. Businesses would stay open late. There were firecrackers and lion dances. I'm not an expert at this art – I can only tell you what I know. The legend of the lion dance is that one day, an unknown creature came out of the mountains and began destroying crops. He was so destructive that the people began to fear starvation – but a heroic lion arrived on the scene and saved the day, fighting the monster and saving the people.

Symbolically, in the Lion Dance, a black lion is considered to be especially skilled and advanced – he's very brave – always ready to fight and stand up for what is right.

Chinese culture is full of symbolism and traditions. Colors are quite symbolic, like the red packets for lucky money. There are traditional things associated with each of the colors.

We still have symbolic meaning hidden in our kung fu forms – For example: most of you have probably seen the left hand clutched around the right fist in greeting – this "soft hand" greeting is a gesture of respect. And by contrast a "hard hand" – with the left hand formed as a knife hand, is a challenge to fight to the death. There are many such symbols, and some of them are secret, even to this day. The movements can only be deciphered by those who are familiar with the meaning.

Lorenzo Lamas & Eric

(Dream)

"Imagination is more important than knowledge." – Albert Einstein

CHAPTER SIX: I Become a World Traveler

    – "The journey of a thousand miles begins with a single step." – Lao Tsu

In 1960, when I was about 14, I began to seek my fortune. In Chinese culture the male role model is that of the breadwinner, and the woman's traditional role is to take care of the husband. The tradition is that the man goes first to pave the way for his family, and the family follows. So as the eldest son, my grandparents expected me to be the breadwinner for the next generation – a tradition in Chinese families. The younger generation is a direct extension of "chi" – their life force... this was expected of me.

My grandfather on my father's side had already moved to the United States – to Oakland – And that move had been fortunate – not only for him, but for ALL my family. Grandfather was the patriarch, the head of our family – He was the real breadwinner,

Lee Family

and his example inspired me a lot in life. He was a very successful man who actually provided a living for five whole generations of Lees. We were very fortunate to have his industry and wisdom, looking after us.

I liked the idea of freedom and economic opportunity that America offered, so that was where I headed. We call America "Gold Mountain" – the term may date back to the early California gold rush days, or it may just be that America had the reputation in those days of being a place to seek your fortune. Freedom is everything. People always want to be free.

And I was fortunate – I had my family's support to give me the mental strength, confidence, and courage I would need for the journey.

> "When I first met Eric, I didn't really know a lot about martial arts. My husband is his student, and I had known Eric mainly as a kind, sweet, friendly, down-to-earth person, whom I had trained with in the park with my husband… And then we went to a black belt event where he was being honored… And he was like a 'rock star' in the martial arts world! EVERYBODY knew him! I had no understanding of all his achievements… And it made me appreciate him even more: He's the same person in front of a group of people that he is one-on-one."
>
> -Sylvia Cranston, black belt, attorney, now a full-time martial arts instructor.

We Chinese are very family oriented, and today we call it that we are "networking", although we didn't have that word back then, to describe our family structure. As a family, we took care of each other –our friends and loved ones. That was how we thought.

In those days Hong Kong was a British Crown Colony, and passports and visas were naturally controlled back by the British colonial government. It's all completely different now, of course, but back then only a few visas to the various ports of call were given out at any one time, so getting this paperwork was a lengthy process.

I wanted to go to America, but to receive a visa to America would have taken forever, so I had to make the trip in stages, coming by an indirect route: It was quite an adventure.

I took the voyage on a big full scale ocean liner – one of a famous line of huge ships called the "President's Line". It was decided that I go by ship, because I could bring more possessions on a ship, than on a plane.

It was like one big floating city – there were games like shuffleboard, a swimming pool, and music… All of which would have been fine, but there was also the ocean itself, and until I got my "sea legs" I became quite seasick. I devised a strategy of staying in the middle of the boat, because it rocked a bit less. It wasn't such a successful strategy, but I had no choice other than to do that, and endure as best I could.   I still have a picture of that boat.

During the trip, I spent 24 hours docked in Tokyo, Japan, and I saw my very first karaoke bar there – Karaoke is now everywhere, of course, but I had never seen or heard of it in China.

To tell the truth, it was my first time in ANY bar, EVER. I went with some other passengers, and nobody asked me my age or anything, so it was fine.

Every seat had its own microphone, and oddly enough, everybody was singing in English. I knew a little English at the time from the British schools I'd attended, but I just sat and listened, and enjoyed the experience.

They brought us food – sushi – and I had my first taste of Japanese food there. Everyone was very polite – bowing to everyone. It was a little awkward for me, because I knew there were still some hard feelings between Japanese and Chinese – a holdover from the war. But everything was fine.

From there we sailed on to Oahu, but we didn't really stay to look around. I didn't see that much of Hawaii during that journey, and I don't remember it that much.

Today, it is one of my very favorite places to visit. Most people think it's expensive – and it is, if you don't know your way around. But if you have contacts on the island it can actually be quite affordable, and there are lots of great fresh-caught seafood – fresh from the ocean. So if you know the island and the people, and have good "people skills," you can still live quite well on very little.

From there the ship docked in San Francisco, the famous city by the Bay. What an amazing experience, seeing the huge Golden Gate Bridge for the first time.

My first image of America, ever, other than those western movies I saw in Hong Kong, was a picture of the Golden Gate Bridge. Grandfather had sent us a picture of it, and suddenly, there it was before me, huge, and grand, and wonderful – the picture had become reality.

Actually, I am the third man of the Lee family to come to America. My father, Shao Nam Lee, attempted the journey, in 1935, and got as far as Angel Island – which was a quarantine facility like the one at Ellis Island on the East Coast, where the Statue of Liberty now stands.

Unfortunately, he was one of the ones who didn't make it in. He and my grandmother spent 18 months there, fighting a legal battle to prove that they were related to my grandfather in Oakland. They were housed with other Asian and European immigrants, all waiting their turn to enter, but it didn't work out, and they were eventually sent back to China.

Angel Island is now open to the public as a sort of memorial to the people who came there looking for a better life in America. I eventually paid $2,500 to get his name on the wall there on Angel Island, and if you ever go there you can see it.

But father didn't get to come here to America until years later. My grandfather, Lum Piu Lee, finally brought him in successfully. He passed away in Oakland in 2015, at the ripe old age of 94 – so he had the last laugh on those people who sent him back to China! My family is very long-lived – my mother, Kwok Wei Lin, passed away in 2017 at 96. So we Lees have good genes I guess; and I'm hoping to be long-lived as well. I hope to live to be a hundred. So far I seem to have a pretty good head start!

It was in San Francisco that I met my grandfather, the patriarch of our family, for the first time. He had already moved there, and was very successful in providing for the Lee family, so meeting him was a big thing for me... Although to a Westerner, you might not have noticed its importance.

In the "old school" of Chinese culture, we don't hug, or kiss our elders, or even talk in their presence most of the time. We are taught to be humble, not expressive. We are taught to listen, only. If we do speak, and we are younger, then out of respect we say, "What can I do for you?" or "How can I help you?" Respect, for us is VERY important.

We Chinese call our elders by their title rather than by their name – so we might say "Father" or "Uncle" or "Grandmother" – but calling them by their name is a "no-no" – disrespectful. The only exception to that was well-known judo and jiu-jitsu man, Wally Jay, who was actually good friends with my grandfather. He always insisted that people call him, "Wally." I studied a little with him, learning some judo.

Grandfather owned Lun Kee Poultry, in Oakland. When it first opened it was exclusively a poultry shop, but later when we moved to a new location, it became a famous restaurant in the

East Bay area. Grandfather also owned a 24-room boarding house, which is where I stayed when I was there. The building is still there in Oakland, at 379 8th Street.

But I wasn't destined to stay in Oakland, that time... I stayed only about two days, because it had been decided that I would go to Nicaragua to stay with friends of his, to make those contacts. So as a dutiful grandson, I followed his wishes.

I went by plane. It was my first time on a plane, but I wasn't scared. Actually, I was the only passenger, and it was quite enjoyable – looking down on the ocean and the land was a new adventure for me.

My grandfather had given me some money, and two nice, roast ducks to take with me for food. Ordinarily, the rules are that the flight attendants don't fraternize with the passengers, but because I was the only passenger, they were friendly, and as I was preparing to eat my roast ducks, I asked them, "Would you like some?" So they sat down and we all enjoyed dinner together. They were happy to have the duck and I was happy to have the company on the long trip, so it was a "win-win" situation.

I stayed in Managua, with my grandfather's friend, Mr. Wong, and lived in his house for 3 months – Wow, was it a fancy place! There were maids, servants, and even a swimming pool. He was politically powerful in that country – he was actually friends with the President of the whole country. The President even came to celebrate Mr. Wong's birthday at his house. He arrived with a huge entourage of armed guards who surrounded the area and even stood on-guard while he was there paying his respects.

Those guards are universal – there has to be tight security for the leader of a country. The story goes that in ancient times, if you had the rare privilege of being bidden to approach the Emperor of China, as a gesture of politeness and respect, when you approached the "Dragon Throne" – that's what they called the Emperor's seat of state – you had to swing your hands in a rapid figure-8 to show that you had no weapons concealed in your sleeves – the figure eight would in theory impart a lot of momentum to any concealed daggers, and they would fly out and clatter to the ground.

That's another one of those "secret" moves that still persists to this day, that you can sometimes see, hidden in the salutation with which Chinese martial arts forms begin. It's a move with a hidden meaning.

There are many such moves in Chinese martial arts forms. The hand-weapon formed with the first and second fingers extended, for example, can indicate a strike at a vital point, or it can suggest a dagger, cleverly concealed by the hand in a reverse grip. The emperor's bodyguards were naturally very aware of these kinds of tricks that might be employed by assassins, and took care to protect him from them at all times.

The protocol or custom back then was that you could not even look directly at the emperor. He would wear a gold-colored robe with a dragon elegantly embroidered on the silk, and the robe would be decorated at the bottom with many silken "dragon's claws" – the more dragon's claws trimming the robe, the higher your rank – But only the emperor could wear gold – it was a color reserved for him.

Again, this was symbolism: In Western mythology, the dragon is a sort of rampaging monster, that the knight in shining armor has to save the girl from… But in Chinese mythology the dragon is a benevolent, immortal, magical creature of immense power and wisdom.

Legend has it that he can become visible or invisible, so you never know just when he is lurking about. And he was supposed to pay special attention to the doings of the Emperor, because the Emperor's actions controlled the destiny of China. So the mythological story goes that the dragon often acted as the Emperor's invisible protector and unseen, ever-present, magical agent.

This modern-day ruler of Nicaragua was a bit less elaborately dressed than the Emperor of ancient times, of course, and if he had any magical dragons lurking around him, I certainly didn't see them. That was a long time ago, and I can't remember now if he wore a suit or a military uniform, but as you can imagine, it was still quite the event, seeing all that take place.

It was 1960, and Chubby Checker and his "Peppermint Twist" were all the rage, even in Nicaragua. I've always enjoyed dancing, and I actually learned to do the "Twist" and the Cha-cha in Managua. I might have liked to have stayed there longer, but at my grandfather's direction I moved to Bluefields, Nicaragua, with another friend of my grandfather's.

"Bluefields" is actually an anglicized Dutch name – "Blauvelt." The place was named after the Dutch pirate Abraham Blauvelt, who would hide his ship in the waters of that bay, during the early 17th Century.

My grandfather's friend owned a huge supermarket store, with many workers, and I lived in a room upstairs. While there, I continued to work on my English, and I had a kind, black lady as a private tutor in the language.

For a reason that I did not know at the time, the black people there spoke English, while the rest of the population spoke Spanish. Later I learned that they spoke English, because originally, they came from the island of St. Vincent where they were kept by the British as slaves. They successfully rebelled against the British slave traders, and escaped from their misery and bondage, to freedom. They migrated to the Honduran coast, and from there to the rest of the Central American coast, which includes Nicaragua.

Nicaragua is a warm, tropical country; very hot and humid; but everything was very inexpensive – so inexpensive it would be hard for most westerners to understand it. In that area at the time, the Chinese were the wealthiest, the natives, second, and the blacks were third, economically.

If you can imagine, the poorest workers would labor three or four days for one package of cigarettes... I'm not sure how they managed to live on that – perhaps they would sell the cigarettes to others, one at a time, as a kind of currency – but I'm speculating. I don't really know how that worked or how they managed to survive on so little.

To give you some idea, a movie there cost 20 cents! I went to a movie there once, and there was even "air conditioning!" Well, sort of... I looked up and there was no roof! Everyone had umbrellas in case it rained! Can you imagine that? A roof was a luxury that the movie-goers didn't have!

One of my friends there was Mr. Fong. He was older than me, and he worked in the market – he was a kung fu man – a White Crane stylist, and that he was like a mentor to me.

He tried to teach me knife throwing, but that didn't work out at all well... We set up a target on the balcony, which turned out not to be a very bright idea:

I threw the knife, and to my horror, I missed the target completely and the knife went sailing over the edge of the balcony and down toward the street!

I ran to the guard rail on the balcony to see what had happened below. Thankfully, nobody down there was hurt, but the blade had somehow smashed the bottle of a drunkard below, just as he was all set to take a drink! Thankfully it missed him entirely.

I reached the balcony's railing just as the drunk looked up in horror, from the smashed wine bottle up to me –

...And if you can imagine the scene, there I was, standing there with all these throwing knives in my hands, looking like some sort of killer fiend from a horror movie. Well, the poor drunken fellow was naturally terrified! He thought that I'd done that on purpose! So he took one look at me and he ran off as fast as if the devil himself was after him! The poor fellow was so drunk that he tripped and fell three times, but he never slowed down for an instant...

I've always felt bad about that...

The place that I lived in above the supermarket, was, well, a bit crude by today's standards. To give you some idea, the "toilet" was positioned over the Lake, with the water only about 5 feet below. Actually, it was a little room with a seat, that had a hole in it. And the fish would actually congregate in the lake below and jump up to eat the... well, you get the idea. ...I suppose it made plumbing a lot simpler, although I don't believe I'd care to fish in those waters.

I enjoyed Bluefield though. There was shooting and hunting... I was about 14 at the time, and there was a beautiful young lady, about 18 or 19 who would always wink at me when I went by. One day as I passed, she picked up her skirt – and she had no underwear... But I was shy, and too young at the time to take things any further, which was probably fortunate...

But there was another young lady whom I was attracted to, and one day I worked up the courage to go and visit her at her house. But when I knocked on the door I heard a strange, high voice say,

"Nobody home!" It was an African Gray Parrot that the family kept! So I missed my chance to get to know her better.

While I was there in Bluefields, I continued with my English studies and also learned some bad Spanish. I stayed in Managua 3 months, and Bluefields for three months – so all-in-all, I spent half a year in Nicaragua. It was quite an adventure for me.

(Confidence)

"Faith is living, daring confidence in God's grace, so sure and certain that a man could stake his life om it a thousand times." – Martin Luther

CHAPTER SEVEN: I Come to America!

"Life is always under construction."

From Bluefields, I finally arrived at my destination in America – Oakland, California. There I was, finally, at home in the fabled land we Chinese call "Gold Mountain." It was quite exciting for me. Grandfather had made his fortune there, and I was confident that I would too!

I went to McChesney Middle School, there in Oakland, in 1960 through 1962, and I soon made my first friend there, an American Chinese named Danny Ma. My favorite teacher was a lady named Mrs. Madow. I always had talent as an artist, and I was the best painter in the class – it was a natural ability.

But it was here that I really got interested in martial arts.

I've already told you about the stupid bully that chopped my neck just for the fun of it, who did almost kill me, and inspired me to get really serious about my martial arts training.

The very next day after my experience with that bully, I went to a Shaolin kung fu school and told the sifu there that I wanted to learn how to fight. And I did, too! I wanted to find the guy who had hurt me and do the same to him. I was angry the whole time I was training – I really had revenge in my heart. But all the teacher did was forms.

Eventually, I studied with 2 or three different instructors there in Oakland – all of whom hated each other for some reason.

Not to digress, but I've always wondered why that attitude was so common in the martial arts – all the hostility and bad feelings between the various styles of Martial Arts. I've never understood that... whether it was that they were insecure or felt threatened, or studied fighting because they didn't have the social skills to talk? ... I don't know. It's STILL a puzzlement to me - I've never been able to understand it. I've always wanted to get along with people. I have friends throughout all the martial arts – it's natural for me, it's not something that I have to work at. And I'm grateful for it – It solves a LOT of problems before they even get started.

I like people, I always have. I'm naturally friendly. If I ask you for lunch, I pay the bill. I like making others happy, because that makes ME happy, and I like to make that first gesture of friendship. Ultimately, that helps me too. We Chinese have a saying: "A clenched fist cannot shake hands."

The saying may come from a story that is popular among practitioners of the Chan sect of Buddhism:

> There was once a man who married a wife who was very ungenerous and tight with money. Although the family did well thanks to his hard work, popularity in the community, and sound business sense, the wife absolutely HATED to spend money, and would never be charitable to others. The man, by contrast, was a generous fellow, and beloved for this quality – which greatly enhanced his success in business... but the wife's constant penny-pinching both made him miserable, and

even affected his business adversely. He and the wife argued constantly about this.

Driven finally to distraction, the husband threw up his hands, and decided to go see a monk; who had a reputation for being very wise; for advice. He went to the monk's temple and complained loud and long about the woman's tight-fisted habits. At first the monk demurred, but the man was so persistent that at last the monk promised to speak to the wife and see what he could do.

Arriving at the man's house he walked up to the wife and bowed, paying his respects.

Knowing that the husband had sent him, the wife tightened her jaw and crossed her arms, ready for any lecture he would make against her miserly habits... but the monk only stood before her quietly and clenched his fist.

"What would you call it if my hand were always like this?" he asked calmly.

The wife shrugged, somewhat confused and taken aback. "Some kind of deformity, or perhaps an old injury, I suppose..." she replied.

The monk then opened his hand flat. "And if it was always like this?" he asked.

"Another kind of deformity or injury," the wife replied.

The monk smiled. "Very good!" he said, "If you understand that, you are a wise person."

And with that, he bowed and walked away, leaving the wife in stunned astonishment.

From that day on, the wife helped the husband distribute wealth as well as receive it.

On the surface, the story is about money, but it's also about rigidity of thought, as opposed to responsiveness and flexibility... give and take, mutual interest, working together with the other person in a constructive manner – taking into account each other's needs and feelings.

We martial artists know that living things are inherently flexible and pliant, whereas in death things become stiff, hard, and rigid. Working and getting along with others is like that too, but sometimes we forget that in dealing with each other.

Each of us has blind spots that others can easily see, but we ourselves cannot see. We are only as good as our weakest link – and we are always in the middle of a blind spot when it comes to seeing ourselves as others see us. It takes courage and humility, but you have to sometimes put ego outside the door and listen.

Different styles, different systems, different teachers... I like to get along with them all, no problem. I wish there could be more of that in the martial arts, and I do all I can to promote the view that we are all brothers and sisters in the martial arts – that our mutual interest in the art that we love should UNITE us, rather than divide us.

But as I've admitted, I've felt those feelings of anger too, so I'm a fine one to talk... As I've said, in those days, I was training for revenge, and I was training HARD – I was really determined to get it one day.

I didn't know anything about tournaments in those early days. I just wanted to be able to defend myself – and of course, I wanted to find the guy that almost killed me and teach him a lesson that he'd never forget.

Hopefully nobody reading these words will ever need that kind of negative "inspiration" – they can just read the book and learn from my mistakes! There's no need to re-invent the wheel.

Negativity like that – holding on to anger – doesn't do anything to the other person that you're mad at, it just makes YOU feel bad... Anger held inside can affect our relationships with others, and it can even make you sick, too, so I don't believe in holding grudges. You have to have the strength to let it go. Negative thoughts can slow you down, or even stop you completely – and they only affect you, not the one you're angry at.

We all make mistakes in life, we are not perfect. I've made plenty of them. The important thing is to take responsibility for them and learn from them, rather than beating yourself up over them. Decision made "back then," before we learned better, were the best we knew how to do at the time... You can't DO "back then" – You can only do NOW.

But even so... As it turned out, that negative experience – getting chopped across the throat by that bully – gave me the inspiration to learn: Every day, as regular as clockwork, I'd go to the gym. And a lot of times the gym would smell like, well, a gym. But for me this was like a signal that it was time to train, to improve, to get down to business. This may sound strange, but I still miss the bad smell of the gym.

At first when I got to Oakland, I hung around with mostly Chinese guys, because my English was not that good and I was shy... My English is still kind of "broken English," as they say, but I do have a good vocabulary and I feel I communicate pretty well. Actually, these days I even THINK in English most of the time – because I'm here, I suppose and I'm interacting mostly in English with other Americans. It's only when I'm in China or interacting and conversing with other Chinese, here, that I start thinking in Chinese again. So that's one way that I've become "Americanized."

Similarly, when I started hanging around martial arts tournaments I got comfortable with other Americans, and saw that they accepted me as one of their own, I started hanging around with everybody. If they were interested to learn, I taught them. And I learned from them, just as they learned from me.

And of course, I had to keep up with my studies. I had a lot of respect for my teachers there – I found that they weren't as strict as their British counterparts in Hong Kong, so I did what they said and did my best to learn. There were no video games in those days to distract me – and in fact there were no computers at all back then... this was way before they became common.

But there were girls!

In high school I started dating a lot of girls – mostly Chinese girls. I've always been very active,. I didn't spend a lot of time at home... and I was never home on Friday or Saturday nights.

I went to Oakland Technical High School, and I cultivated a "pompadour" hair style – like Elvis. We dressed "gangster style,"- I couldn't afford one of those leather motorcycle jackets with all the buckles and the stars on the epaulettes like the one in the old Marlon Brando movie – but I wore pleated pants and bell bottoms with wide belts that were all the rage at the time.

Years later, I created my own line of fine, embroidered leather jackets – they're a lot different from the common leather motorcycle jackets that I couldn't afford as a kid, of course – they're modern and very fashionable... nowhere near a motorcycle jacket – but I designed them, and they're quite popular, so now I can afford to have a leather jacket of my own. I have to say, that's a good feeling.

Oakland has a well-deserved reputation for being a "tough" place, today. It was tough even in those days, and there were a lot of fights in high school – serious fights with chains and knifes, but thankfully there were no guns back then. People had them, of course – there were no gun laws like there are today, and they were quite cheap by today's standards – anyone could buy one by mail order. But for unknown reasons they simply were not used.

I had a Filipino friend named Wally, and he and I got into a lot of fights there... It got so bad that I had to change schools to Oakland High School – I liked that school a lot better. There was less violence and I could concentrate more on books than on fighting.

I have to confess, in high school I was not the best student, but I stuck with it. I graduated from Oakland High School in 1966. That school is still there, still teaching kids today.

After I graduated high school, I attended Laney Community College, in Oakland. I studied philosophy there, which I liked. Truthfully, though, I was more interested in cars, girls, and martial arts –not necessarily in that order – than I was in philosophy.

That was an amazing time in the San Francisco Bay area. There were lots of hippies in Berkeley, and of course there was Haight Ashbury, and 1967 was the famous "Summer of Love!" I was actually there!

What a place it was in those days! There were hippies, love beads, Black Panthers, Hell's Angels... Groups like Jimmy Hendrix, The Rolling Stones, and Tower of Power, all played music there.

I also dated a lot. My first American blond girl was a young lady named Shirley.

It was an experience for me, dating an American girl. I guess you could say they were "exotic" to me in a way – They looked different, and talked differently... So I learned from her and she learned from me. She was my first "puppy love." That kind of love, when everything is new to you, it's quite magic. It's like the old song, "This Magic Moment" - which is still a favorite of mine... For me it captures that strange, amazing, awkward-but-wonderful feeling of first love...

Those were the days in the East Bay area! There were many drive-ins, famous hangouts like Mel's Drive in. On Friday and Saturday nights we would all cruise on East 14th St., and San Leandro Street, with loud glass pack hot rods, and drive-ins, martial arts, girls in their cars and on the sidewalk... Everything a young man could possibly ask for! It was such a time, I can tell you!

But life wasn't all play. I wound up getting a degree in auto mechanics – not exactly a "highbrow" intellectual pursuit, but I found it quite useful and practical, and profitable, too... as you'll see!

Eric Lee with Morgan Fairchild

(Balance)

"Life is like riding a bicycle. To keep your balance, you must keep moving." – Albert Einstein

CHAPTER EIGHT: Cars, Cars, and More Cars...

–"She's my Little Deuce Coupe! You don't know what I drive..." – The Beach Boys, 1963

I admit it, as a young man, I had a real "thing" for cars. Cars have gotten me into more trouble than the Martial Arts ever did, which is saying something, when you think about it... And they have almost been the death of me on more than one occasion.

In 1968, I was driving on the Nimitz Freeway in Oakland, and I barely managed to avoid a head-on collision with a drunk who had passed out behind the wheel. Others weren't so lucky. A whole bunch of cars crashed and even rolled over. It was a VERY close call and I was in shock... I had to park the car and wind down... I was lucky to be alive.

As I've told you, I had a degree in auto mechanics, remember, and in those days I LOVED to build hot rods. My first car was a 1957 De Soto with push-button drive and – believe it or not – NO reverse! If we drove it to a place that we had to back out of, it was necessary to get out and push the car, until it was headed in the right direction. I spent $350 dollars to take it to a transmission shop to get it fixed, but the shop was no good, and reverse still didn't work right.

I was in that Desoto, going to the Bay Bridge with my grandma and grandpa in the back, one day – And of course, cars back then had no seatbelts. It had been raining, and the road was wet, and I must have hit a patch of oil or something, because suddenly, we were hydroplaning down the freeway, and the car spun 180 degrees, ZOOP! Just like that - I didn't have a move! One moment I was headed calmly down the highway, straight as an arrow, and the next we were all faced the opposite direction! But fortunately, we didn't hit anything and we were all okay. Which was lucky... We could easily have all been killed.

Experiences like that didn't stop me from my fascination with cars though. The faster they were, the better I liked them!

Eventually I got a '55 Chevy with a big, hot, 327 Corvette engine and a Hurst T-shifter – it was one FAST car. And I'd take it to the Fremont race track, to race it, which was a so much fun. I enjoyed that a lot. Street racers call cars like that "sleepers" – they may LOOK just like your father's calm, sedate, everyday Chevrolet, but under the hood, WOW! - Anything but!

I loved to drive in those days... I drove all over, but had only one accident which was not my fault – Somebody ran a stop sign and grazed my bumper, but thankfully nobody got hurt. My martial arts skills always served me well, driving in Los Angeles. I saved myself from about 5 accidents because of my quick reactions.

I wish I was as good at avoiding tickets! I got 21 of them as a young man, before I learned to keep my foot off the accelerator. My first ticket, the cop pulled me over and I offered him money – because that was the way things were done back in the places I'd lived before, outside the US. The judge asked me about that, and I told him truthfully, that this was the standard custom where I was from – Thankfully, the judge was kind, and he realized that I was telling the truth, and didn't know any better, so he let me go.

Another time I had a '56 Chevy that I'd fixed up, and I was out picking fruit for my uncle, who had an orchard in Sacramento – He was growing pears and peaches there. So I was driving on the property and suddenly I realized I had made a wrong turn and found myself running over a bunch of big pipes that pumped irrigation water, before I could get the car stopped.

Each one of those pipes is quite expensive – they cost like $100 bucks apiece, and I ran over a BUNCH of them. Well, I lost control of the car, and I hit a wall, and the wall collapsed on the car. It cost Uncle thousands of dollars to fix my blunder. I was in big trouble with him that day, I can tell you.

In 1969 and '70, I went up to Coquille, British Columbia, near Vancouver, and stayed with another one of my uncles for about a year. I trained, and taught a bit, and I played a lot of chess with a friend of mine, Alan Ng.

I and two other friends of mine, Aaron and Sam, needed money, so we came up with a plan: With my auto mechanics degree, I knew how to fix up cars, as you know; and Aaron and Sam were natural salesmen. So we figured that we could capitalize on these skills. What could be more natural?!

So we would find a likely looking car, and make a deal with the owner to fix it up and sell it. That was how we did it. And it worked well, too.

Over the course of time I had a '65 Corvette, a Porshe Targa, a Karmann Ghia, a Cadillac, 2 Mercedes, an MG-A, several Mustangs and BMW's... even a Volkswagen "Bug," which I gave to a girlfriend. One car that we got was a really nice one – a 1967 Supersport Camaro 350. Back in those days, we bought it for a just a couple thousand bucks... Now they want $100,000 or more for those cars!

It took time to fix them all up, of course, and so many had accumulated at one point, that I actually found a homeless guy squatting in one of them. I said, "What are you doing here?" And he told me, "I live here." And I was like, "What do you mean you live here? This is MY CAR!" We had so many at the time that I didn't even know he had moved in!

One car I had was a tiny little Honda 3 cylinder... As a joke, my friends picked it up and put the car on the sidewalk. I came out and was like, "WHAT HAPPENED????" Of course they were waiting for this reaction, and they all had a good laugh at my expense.

Sometimes, though, the joke was on the other guy: One time, when I was living in Hollywood, I had just come back from some event or other – a tournament, a demo, who knows what – But for once, I was dead tired. I mean, just EXHAUSTED... Which is rare for me, but it happened.

I was so beat I could hardly keep my eyes open... I made it home to my house, which at the time was at 2158 North Ivar Street. And I just parked my car there on the street and sat there for a while, trying to work up the energy to move.

Ordinarily, tiredness is like dirt: Usually, we can just wash it off. But not this time. This time, I was too tired even to go inside... Finally, I decided to heck with it: I just flopped over into the back seat and went to sleep right there – Boom. Done. Out like a light.

Well, there I was, sleeping peacefully as a baby – not a care in the world, when much to my surprise, a couple of thieves popped open the unlocked door, and tried to steal my radio.

Unfortunately for them, they didn't know I was there in the back seat – they didn't check: Big mistake on their part.

No, I didn't hurt them! I'll bet you thought that you were going to hear some sort of dramatic kung-fu war story, about me heroically beating up all the bad guys with my fancy martial arts moves, didn't you?

Well you're not! – Sorry to disappoint you, but it wasn't necessary! This is what I did:

Breaking into my car uninvited and stealing my radio wasn't nice, of course, and there I was, watching it happen. Well, that wouldn't do...

...So, without warning I exploded up from the back seat, making what I hoped was a horrible face and twisting my hands into claws, growling and screaming like a banshee:

> "I've known Eric since he was 16. I watched him grow from a young kid with talent to an adult, watched him mellow out, become a young man, and take on his adult persona. He does beautiful kata, as everyone knows. He's skilled and well-coordinated, but he's also thoughtful, outgoing, and friendly, too."
>
> -Leo Fong, member, Black Belt Hall of Fame, tournament promoter, filmmaker, and retired Methodist minister

"BRAAAAOORRRRRAH!!!!!!!!!!!!!" Like that!

Boy, were they surprised! "Terrified," might be a better word, I suppose... Those guys fled so fast they even forgot to take my radio with them. They ran so quick you could actually see them getting smaller as they raced away down the street. That was my kung-fu for that moment. You don't always have to beat people up to win. Sometimes getting creative and doing the unexpected is a lot more fun.

(God)

"With God, all things are possible." – Matthew 19:26

CHAPTER NINE: Martial Arts, Martial Arts, and MORE Martial Arts!

"Experience is a stepping stone to go on to the next level."

While going to school in Oakland, I became the president of the Laney Martial Arts Club – As I've said, at the time I was a real fanatic in training. We'd all get together and share our knowledge: Judo, Aikido, chin na, wrestling, boxing – whatever. We would get together and exchange tips: I wanted to learn everything. The bigger the arsenal I had, the better I liked it.

I studied with everybody that I could. At the same time we had the martial arts club, I was studying Bruce Lee's concepts with James Yimm Lee, Judo with Wally Jay, and Hung Gar style with Lum Cho. I studied with so many people that it's hard to remember them all. If they wanted to teach it, I wanted to learn it ALL.

At that time I met Al Dacascos for the first time. He was demonstrating defense against multi-man attacks of perhaps as many as 15 or 20 guys. Anybody who has seen one of his demonstrations back then can tell you how impressive they were. I took one look at what he was doing and I said to myself, "THERE!!!! THAT's what I want!" So I began studying with him.

Sifu Al's Won Hop Kune Do is an offshoot from Professor Adriano Emperado's Kajukenbo System - a "softer," more "Chinese" style Than Professor Emperado's Kajukenbo system – Kajukenbo is a "harder" style – more like Ed Parker's Kenpo Karate.

Eric & Sifu Al Dacascos

It was Sifu Al who encouraged me to participate in tournaments: He was a great competitor himself, and he was the one who got me started in competition.

Bruce Lee was in Oakland at that time too, of course, and Sifu Al and Bruce were friends. Bruce wasn't famous back then – he was just one of the "other" kung fu instructors in town... People always ask me if I'm related to Bruce Lee – I'm not, so far as I know, but I tell them, "Yes! 2000 years ago!" Who knows! If it isn't true it oughta be! :)

I really wanted to learn how to FIGHT. I'd watch those two move and they were both so FAST, with so much power. I wanted to be like them.

One time though, I got to see a higher level of skill from them: One of Bruce's students and one of Al's students got into a fight, so as instructors they had to meet over tea to talk about it.

These kinds of things can be quite serious, because in the old days in China, if the students had a problem, the TEACHERS would fight. That was the custom. And there could be feuds and bad blood between the schools from then on... But Bruce and Al were friends, and they decided – wisely, I feel – that their students' problem was just between the students, so they stayed friends. I think that is a much better way to handle it. Nobody EVER wins a fight. Even if you win, you lose.

While I was training in Oakland, I saw my first martial arts "gi" – the heavyweight cotton uniform that all martial artists wore in those days. I walked into the gym and I took one look at all those white uniforms – and you see, in China, white is symbolically a color associated with mourning – and the first thought that popped into my head was, "Who died?"

Even uniforms were different back then. Today nice uniforms are easy to get – even stylish ones, of just about any color you can imagine – but back then about the only thing that was commonly available were those heavyweight white judo gi's with the short, calf-length pants.

You could wash the gi, but if you washed the belt it would shrink up to nothing! It would become so short that you couldn't even tie it around your waist. So you didn't wash the belt.

Actually, that's how the whole "black belt" thing got started – or so I'm told. Because you couldn't wash the belt, it would get darker and darker, the longer you were there. So over time, the senior students and instructor's belts became dark black. They'd say, "Don't wash your belt!!! You'll wash the knowledge out!" Strictly speaking that's not true, of course, but you'd surely shrink it up so much that you couldn't wear it.

So as you can see, the simple belt and gi that we had back then weren't very stylish. Today style is more interesting to me. I'm still an artist and a calligrapher, and I like to create things, like the embroidered leather jacket that I mentioned before.

Style didn't interest me much back then, though – although It did some! I bought my kung fu uniforms that I wore in competition, so that I would stand out from the other competitors – It's important to stand out, as long as it's in a good way. A lot of other competitors followed my style in this, so I started a trend.

But mostly, back then all I wanted to do was train extra hard to beat the other styles.

Martial artists refer to those days as the "Golden Age" of tournament. It was quite a time. Chuck Norris, Mike Stone, and Joe Lewis were the "Big 3" winning all the fighting. There were big, major tournaments, networked all across the country that we competitors would all attend. There were demonstrations by the masters and practitioners of various styles, and breaking competitions.

California was a real Mecca for the martial arts in those days, and the CKC championships were, in my opinion, the best of the best. To this day I still feel that the CKC championship was the most demanding and difficult tournament ever – I have to say, it was even better than the nationals. We would have the tournaments at the Civic Auditorium in San Francisco – Ralph Castro, a strong Kajukenbo stylist and a student of the famous Professor K.S. Chow – Ed Parker's teacher - ran the event.

The tournaments at that time came before the invention of the safety equipment that you see today – Bare knuckles! There were no gloves and no protectors – back then they depended on razor sharp control and good will... A well-trained martial artist could come within a fraction of an inch of your face, without ever touching you, and for many, perfect control was a matter of pride. Those punches would come so close to the face that you could feel the wind from them. That kind of precision control is rare today.

The rules were that you couldn't make contact to the face... You would get disqualified if you did. To the body? Well, it tended to be pretty hard contact and you had to be in good shape.

Some of the competitors then were pretty ruthless, though – they would make REALLY hard contact, figuring that it was worth the loss of a point to intimidate the other guy for an easy win.

One of the competitors, I forget who, called them "promise tournaments" – "I promise I won't hit you if you promise you won't hit me." And as the action got more intense, the amount of contact tended to ratchet-up too. So as you can imagine, with two strong fighters, competition could get pretty fierce.

The first tournament I won was the California Karate Championships, which we called "CKC." I was only a green belt back then, really, but I always competed in the black belt division – kung- fu doesn't emphasize rank like karate and other martial arts do, or it didn't back then, so that's what I did. I went where the competition was the best.

I still think that the CKC competition was consistently the best and toughest of any tournament I've ever participated in. The first time I competed, I swept the whole event, winning fighting, form, and weapons. I took home six trophies that day, winning everything clean.

From there it seems I went to every tournament that there was – the Internationals, the Central North American Championships in Albuquerque, Battle of Atlanta in Georgia, St. Louis… everywhere. It was exciting for me, and I was really DRIVEN to win – I was a real fanatic about winning. Back in those days people mostly did karate – kung-fu was rare, but I didn't care about styles, I felt I had to beat the competition no matter what – beat them at THEIR game.

I started teaching about that time, at the YWCA in Oakland. It was a good deal for me – about 70% of the publicity and rent was taken care of by them – and I had many students. One of the students, a Filipino woman, named Maria, was accosted on the street by 2 muggers. She was only 16, but boy, she was tough! She knocked both men out!

I was challenged once there, by a boxer who didn't believe that my kung-fu was effective – I don't like to fight, but I felt I had no choice. I beat him with one punch – I "lap-saoed" his hand as he punched – it's a wrist-grabbing technique – and simultaneously punched him near the back of the jaw, just in front of the mandible.

They're not used to being grabbed like that — it's not in their rules, and they're wearing big gloves when they fight, so they don't tend to encounter that kind of technique, and their reflexes tend not to be trained to deal with it — that's what I mean about the difference between sport fighting and real fighting where there are no rules and no pads. He became my student.

In Oakland challenges like that were pretty common at the time, but thankfully, that's no longer the custom.

It was about then that I got my first press exposure in the Oakland Tribune — in that first article I had my back facing the camera — I was shy, and embarrassed to have that kind of attention. But, I had to learn to get over that.

I started doing a lot of demonstrations and seminars at about that time. Because I trained so hard, I had good form and technique, and I was becoming very well known, so a lot of people came.

> "Eric Lee is my sifu — my teacher. I've known him since I was a kid... He's been my mentor since I was 14. He's a great teacher — The greatest guy in the world — Humble... calm... I've never seen him angry. I've been put in the Black Belt Hall of Fame but he still teaches me today. He's always helping someone. He's a LEGEND, and a fine man."
>
> - Robert Dixon, black belt, longtime Eric Lee Student

I learned to stand OUT in competition. You HAVE to stand out. If you're just average, if you look like everybody else, you're gonna lose.

And similarly, if you look at somebody competing and think, "wow, he has a better kick than me" – negative thoughts like that, you already lost. Your mind has to be strong, and you have to have worked that form into your being so many times that it's a part of you, so that a mistake is impossible. A lot of competitors you see haven't done that preparation – they're still thinking about what move comes next and not making a mistake – that's wrong:

Even when I wasn't training in the gym, I would use visualization, I would close my eyes and visualize each move. I don't even DREAM that I will be losing any tournament. Negative thoughts can slow you down or stop you completely.

For each event I would prepare 4 or five different forms that I can do really well – preparation like that is crucial, just so you have a selection if somebody does the same form, or you feel you need something different – and that thoroughness and extra attention to detail gives you a subtle, but real mental edge over the other competition.

And one other little tip, for you competitors out there: I always preferred to go last, if I had a choice – then I could SEE what my competition is. I prepared my mind to be very strong. Many competitors neglect this aspect of training, but it's very, very important.

A tournament is an opportunity to show your style, your showmanship, your speed, grace, and power. There's no time to think about form when you are performing – You have to KNOW what you are doing to the point that you don't even have to think about it – the form should be so practiced that it is second-nature to you, just as natural as breathing. That way you're free to project your energy to the audience.

When you perform, you have to be powerful, confident, EXPLOSIVE – you have to OWN the stage. There can be no doubt that you are the champion. You have to FEEL like you are going to win. You have to stand out, be unique – in a good way. The beginning, the middle, and the end of the form all have to be powerful, with no flaw.

Those are important keys to success. They are all in the mind first, and in the body second, from doing all that work, and that makes a real difference.

And there is one other important thing: Drawing energy from the audience. A lot of people are actually afraid of the audience, but I'm not.

I have no stage fright. How can I? Many people may not understand this, but to a real performer, the audience is actually an asset – a luxury, even, like a fine musical instrument – you can actually tap into their energy and use it to make your performance better, make your form more aesthetic.

Using the audience makes your projection and your showmanship far better than it could ever be alone – all those people give you inner strength. Nobody wants to go to a performance and have a BAD time, right? So they are all sitting there hoping that you will succeed, knock it out of the park, dazzle them and make them feel great – make them feel glad that they came!

So if you understand that truth, the audience is there to help you out, even if they don't know it.

That's an important lesson for a competitor or a performer to know.

And think about it: Even if you wanted to, you couldn't PAY all those people to sit there in the stands watching you – you couldn't afford it! So it's a real privilege to perform in front of an audience – a great opportunity! There's no point whatsoever in being scared of it.

I trained REALLY HARD for those tournament. Actually, I have to confess, I OVER-trained - BADLY. In those days I would train 6 or 7 hours a day, which is too much! I didn't know as much about training and health as I do today. Rest for the body is actually as important as training.

But in those days I was so enthusiastic that I didn't know balance. Balance in life is important - If you train hard you also have to take a good vitamin and herb regimen and get enough rest so that the body can replenish and repair itself. That's essential to health.

And of course, you should ALWAYS avoid things like stimulants and so-called "recreational" drugs. Too much of anything is not good for you. Overtraining, overworking overeating – things like that are not good - everything has to be done in balance. As with all things, it's a balance of yin and yang.

Some things I did right, though. When I was eating for competition I'd take wheat germ oil, and have a big bowl of white rice with soy sauce – I grew up with that! I'd take brewer's yeast for endurance. I never EVER did drugs or steroids – those things will kill you.

To build up my wind, I'd do a 100 yard dash FAST, then I'd walk back, relaxed, and then I'd do it all over again. And I developed the habit of running up and down the stadium steps at my high school, putting an even greater edge on my endurance, which was already very good.

In addition to training hard at the martial arts, I started to play plenty of basketball at Lincoln Recreation center, Oakland. I was hoping to grow taller and be able to jump high – now I know that that it is the mind, and not the body that allows you to jump high. If you train hard and put your body in perfect position with each movement, and move explosively, up you go!

Eric Lee & Gene LaBelle

Eric Lee & Bill "Superfoot" Wallace

(Discipline)

"True discipline gives enthusiastic obedience to instructions even though they do not satisfy the reason."
M. K. Gandhi

CHAPTER TEN: My "Other Sports..."

"Would you like to ride, in my beautiful balloon?" – **The Fifth Dimension, "Up, Up, and Away!"**

I've always been an active person – VERY active. I can't help it. So I enjoy different sports.

In addition to martial arts, I also did gymnastics, and weight lifting with light weights. On the lighter side of exercise, I did some waterskiing and snow skiing; and I enjoyed things like swimming, camping, horseback riding, and jogging, and hiking. I love to hike and explore new places.

Dune buggies! Now THERE'S a thrill! My friend Michael Armstrong introduced me to them out in Oregon, and now I love them too! They combine my love of cars and exploring, all at once. Some of the newer ones have absolutely AMAZING suspension – they can take a rugged mountain trail and make it feel almost like a trip down a neighborhood street...

How they do it, I can't imagine, but they do, and the know-how that goes into designing a setup like that must be absolutely stunning. It's a feat of engineering, and as someone who knows a thing or two about suspension, from my training with cars, I really respect the achievement.

But not all vehicles I've ridden in have suspension, though, or even wheels, or steering, for that matter! How's that possible? I'm glad you asked:

Once when I was in Albuquerque I got to ride in a hot air balloon. They held the First World Hot Air Balloon Championships there in 1973, and at the same time the Central North American Championships, which I attended, were going on. So I met some balloonists and I got invited up. It was an adventure and a new experience, and I like both. So I said yes!

It's an amazing experience – unique, really. The takeoff isn't abrupt or shocking; it's nothing like a plane or a helicopter... It's unexpectedly "soft". You just sort of drift upward, like... nothing. It's very deceptive, in a way... You just float up quietly. So quietly that you don't fully realize what's happening...

...Until all of a sudden, there you are, 100 feet up, going "Wow, I REALLY am committed, here, aren't I?" Of course, by that time it's too late to change your mind and get out. :)

And as I said, there's no steering wheel: You can't just get in one and fly over to the next town... Most people don't understand that those things basically go wherever the wind takes you. You don't really get to decide where you're going – the wind does that.

And the really odd thing is, there ISN'T any sensation of wind up there because you're ONE with the wind, moving with it, drifting on the air currents. Of course, wind CAN be a factor, which is why balloonists typically fly in the mornings before the sun heats the air up and creates potentially strong currents - Updrafts, downdrafts, gusts... that sort of thing.... which can be dangerous when you encounter them unexpectedly.

But the point is that you don't have the option of "left" or "right," like you do with a car – just "up" and perhaps most significantly, "DOWN."

There are crews below in cars, that follow the direction of the balloons always keeping the balloon in sight and driving like wild men, trying to stay up with it, because they have to be there when the balloon lands, and if it gets lost, well, that's a problem... at the very least it means that the pilot and passengers may be in for a long walk. And it was especially a problem back then, before cell phones and GPS. So it a big responsibility, and those crews have my respect, because their job may be more risky than the people up in the balloon – there are more objects to run into, downstairs.

Once the balloon lands safely, they're responsible for laying the balloon out and carefully folding it up, and for carrying the basket or "gondola" back to the car.

...And then there's a little thing called "terminal descent." Sound ominous, right? Well it is.

Basically, the "balloon" is a tough, heavy, nylon bag, that gets filled with hot air – exactly like a giant, Chinese sky lantern – and because the air in the envelope - the "balloon" part of the craft – is hotter, it becomes more buoyant – heat rises, right? And that carries the balloon up into the air. And the basket or gondola that the people ride in is attached to the balloon by an intricate series of strong ropes and netting that holds it all in place.

 The pilot pulls a cord that releases a gigantic blast of fire a couple of feet wide and a yard or more long – Think of it as being like a flamethrower going off with a great big roar, just a few feet over your head. That really gets your attention, the first few times he does that, I can tell you! But gradually you get used to it.

The hot air that powers this whole event comes from a thing called the "burner" – which is well-named, because boy does it BURN... And the burner runs on a metal bottle or tank full of propane...

And when you're drifting along, the course that the wind takes you may surprise you by not offering any landing spots, so you may be forced to use more propane than you intended to.

If you run out of propane, while you're looking in vain for a good, safe place to land, well... the air in the envelope cools and you're going downstairs: "Terminal descent" – get it?

Thankfully it doesn't happen all at once. But the problem is that once it starts to happen, you don't have any control over where you come down:

That's called, "gravity" – and it's not just an idea, It's the law. Congress didn't pass that law, and neither did Sir Isaac Newton: Nature did. – Newton just discovered it when an apple fell on his head... Which illustrates the kinds of problems you might encounter with the experience.

You see, nature has its own ideas about how to get things done. So at least from the perspectives of the human beings messing with Mother Nature in order to get that contraption airborne, it can be a bad law, if, for example you come down in the trees, or on top of a church steeple, or in the middle of a river...

Even if you DO have plenty of petroleum in the tank, it takes approximately 15 seconds for the balloon to start going UP, after the pilot pulls the cord that sends a giant blast of flame out, and heats the air inside the balloon hotter, which lifts the balloon higher.

That may not seem like a long time, but there are these things called "power lines" – and they can be HARD to see in the air. So if you're descending, and also being blown toward the power lines, you've got a real potential problem, because not only can the balloon get snagged, or tip over when it hits those lines, but they're also filled with massive amounts of electricity, which can potentially get you fried, just like going to the electric chair. That's not good.

So ballooning can be an adventure. The pilots are carefully trained and licensed for lighter-than-air craft, and a good pilot pays careful attention to the amount of propane he has left and also to the terrain, so that he can plan out a nice, flat place to land – sometimes a park or a big lawn, or a flat meadow or a farmer's empty field – before "terminal descent."

He might be running low on propane and see a good landing spot in the distance, and hit the burner to take the balloon higher in the hope that he'll reach that spot – basically going up with a view toward going down to a nice, flat, safe place to land. So he's always got to be thinking ahead. He relies on his experience to get himself, his passengers, and the balloon, down in one piece. But there's always an element of risk involved.

And even under ideal conditions, a balloon landing can be quite a surprise for the bystanders below. So that's what I did, and it was such an experience.

When you get up there, the old Fifth Dimension song, "Up, Up, and Away" pops into your head almost automatically – you can't help yourself – and it's incredibly peaceful up there – not a sound... not even the faintest breeze... nothing but blue sky and open space.... And seeing the world below so tiny and seemingly peaceful, tends to put your problems in a brand new perspective. So I liked that.

Another sport that I enjoy, which is thankfully a bit less dramatic than hot air ballooning, is fishing. I fished as a child, and I still enjoy it.

Michael Armstrong took me fishing in Oregon once – and I got a nibble! But I was a little over excited and jerked too hard on the line, and pulled the fish's lips off – which couldn't have been any fun for the fish, but then, it was probably better for him than the alternative of getting cooked and eaten.

In any case, I made the mistake of putting too much energy on the line, and he got away; and the next day when I went out to try again, Michael had put up a nice sign which read: "Eric Lee's Lipless Fishing Lake."

So that joke was on me.

Another time I went fishing in Alabama, with my friend, Sid Campbell. We went out for 9 straight days but we caught no fish – not a one! So I finally got frustrated and went out and BOUGHT some fish, and

> "Eric Lee... There's no finer human being alive. I don't think he'd ever been salmon fishing before I took him out. He'd lay out in the back of the boat, and when he got a nibble he'd get surprised and excited, and all that energy and focus would come out... I'd go, 'Eric... GENTLE tug, GENTLE tug!' For me he's a brother from another mother. I'm not really a martial artist, but I met him at a law enforcement seminar in Coos Bay, Oregon., and we got to talking and hit it off. Once we started talking he became my personal friend. He's always calling to see how I am and asking advice on this and that. He's got a great, great heart."
>
> -Michael Armstrong, law enforcement professional.

declared victory as the king fisherman of the whole trip: And I WAS, too. I just went fishing with dollars instead of a rod and reel. Hey, whatever works.

One of my favorite ways to train in Oakland was running around Lake Merritt. I still like Lake Merritt for walks. It's quiet and peaceful. There are geese, and gulls, and beautiful, proud, Snowy Egrets with amazing bright eyes...

There is a remarkable Bonsai tree museum there, too, with dozens of fantastic miniature trees, some of them over a century old. I think one of them has survived in that little pot it lives in for more than 400 years. It was there long before I arrived, and hopefully it will be there long after I leave. If you ever go to Lake Merritt, that place is a "must-see!"

So there are a lot of great experiences to enjoy at Lake Merritt.

But one day when I was there, it wasn't such a great experience. I had learned Praying Mantis double swords from a friend, and I had a pair of swords – they were REAL swords, sharp and quite heavy, and I got up early – 3AM – and went off to train with them at Lake Merritt. I had practiced for a couple hours or more, and enjoyed the dawn, and was walking back to my car when I saw a little baby blackbird on the ground who had fallen from his nest... And I picked him up, intending to help him out, and maybe see if I could find the nest he had fallen out of, and put him where he belonged. But that good intention turned out to be a BIG mistake.

Suddenly, to my surprise, the whole sky filled with big blackbirds. There were so many all at once that they literally darkened the sky, and they ALL attacked me, all at once! It was like Alfred Hitchcock's "The Birds" – but for real.

So I was off and running, trying to protect my eyes, flailing around with the swords, trying to get away and keep all those birds off of me... My hands were bleeding, my face was bleeding, I lost my swords... Finally I got to my car, but the windows were down, and they actually followed me inside, attacking me all the time...

Finally I realized what the problem was and I tossed the little bird I'd been carrying out the window, and managed to get away. It wasn't the gentlest way to handle it, but I was desperate, and it was the best I could do at that moment! You think birds can't fight, and are little – and that's true, but a whole bunch of little things make one BIG thing. It sounds funny to say it now, but those birds really beat me up good.

Thankfully, I did better against humans. In those days we did lots of tournaments and lots of demonstrations with Sifu Al, and I felt like I had finally arrived – I was finally doing what I wanted to do, winning lots of championships.

At the time I was working as a busboy at Jack London Square, at the Seafood Grotto Restaurant, and shortly after that I became a manager at my grandfather's restaurant, Lun Kee, in Chinatown, Oakland. It was a family business – my uncle was the chef.

There were numerous tournaments in the area then, and because I worked there at Lun Kee, and was very well known at the time – and of course, because the food was good – it became the hangout for all the martial arts guys.

Among them, the place was thought of as "Eric Lee's restaurant" – but it wasn't really mine, it was grandfather's – I just worked there, managing the place and making sure that the customers were happy and things were running smoothly.

Everybody's been there at one time or another – Ed Parker, Professor Adriano Emperado, everybody you can imagine. For those martial artists who knew their way around, it was "the happening place to go!" The customers' names often read like a "who's who" of martial arts.

Ed Parker & Eric Lee

Usually that was fine, all the martial artists being there, because it brought in a lot of customers – good for business, you know... It got to the point that about a third of all the customers were all my martial arts friends from the tournaments in the area! I had actually become a "draw," for the business, so that was good... usually...

But one day, a whole team of Japanese guys dressed as samurai – wearing swords and helmets and everything - walked into the place... Like a scene out of a movie! Well the customers didn't know what was happening and it scared them to death.

Everybody left in a hurry without paying. So that was pretty embarrassing.

I had an abundance of trophies that I displayed there – I literally won hundreds of them – Basically, they're hard to dust. Today, I have long since given them all away to other people, but back then it seemed the thing to do, to put them out where people could see... One of my trophies featured a guy with a big, high side kick, and we put it near the kitchen... and eventually the heat from the kitchen melted that high side kick down to a low shin kick – it was very amusing!

We didn't always go to Lun Kee, though... When I was in L.A. we'd go to the Golden Dragon Restaurant in Chinatown – they had great dim sum there... Actually dim sum is a breakfast meal in China - a chance for friends to get together in the mornings to be sociable. But here in the 'States, Americans didn't know that, and the Chinese here naturally responded to the customer demand for dim sum at any time of the day – So here in America it's breakfast all the time: What a country!!!

"Dim sum," roughly translated, means "Point to your heart's desire," which is basically what you do – It's how you order. They have waitresses walking by with various tempting breakfast treats that the chef has prepared, and you simply point to what you want to eat, and they bring it to you – the menu is also the meal.

I love to eat - I've always had a huge appetite – I still do – (Shhhh!!! Don't tell people that, I won't get invited to dinner!), and I love socializing with friends, so this combines two of my favorite pastimes. I still love to do that.

It was at about that time that I met my good friend Sid Campbell. Sid has since passed away, and I miss him to this day. What a great guy he was!

Sid was doing Tiburo Nakasato's Shorin Ryu style at his school on Maple Street. I had done a demonstration at the Oakland Museum, and Sid came and introduced himself as the head of museum security... Actually, I found out later that he was the only security man there – so he was both the general and the army, all in one.

He was a big guy, very tough looking... and he gave me a card, and introduced himself, and said "Why don't you come by my school and see me."

Dumb me, I thought he was challenging me! I actually thought he wanted to fight, which may give you some idea of the social climate in Oakland at the time. So, I figured "Ok, well..." and I showed up there. I wasn't going to be the one to show fear.

He invited me inside, and I actually made him go in first. I thought, if he moves, I'm gonna hit him first, but he reached out and said, "Eric! Have a beer!" And he handed me a "cold one." Well, that was a relief! He wanted to be friends!

Eric, Kay, Sid Campbell, Dianne, Ted, Gerald Okamura

That was Sid – very charismatic, a lot of fun, a lot of jokes. I sure do miss him.

That's one tough thing about getting older... I've always made it a point to know a lot of people and have a lot of friends - I have about 20,000 addresses in my book. So many! Knowing and interacting with people means that you enjoy their company, and also that business opportunities tend to present themselves, too. But the downside to that, at my age is that friends sometime pass away... Ninety friends of mine have passed on before me. Some of them got to live their dreams, some did not.

Everybody has dreams, but they don't take action on those dreams, and carry them into the grave. All those friends gave me experiences and shared their lives with me. They made my life fuller and richer. My wish is that I join them later... but for now I'm still here, so I try to take that lesson to heart, enjoy that gift of life, and live it to the fullest.

That is the way of life, too.

Carter Wong & Eric Lee

Peter Kwong & Eric Lee

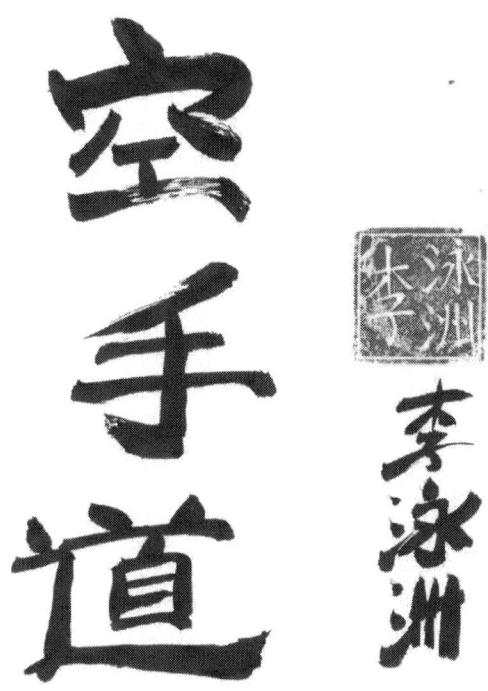

(Karate)

"The ultimate aim of the art of karate lies not in victory or defeat, but in perfection of the characters of its participants." – Master Gichin Funakoshi

CHAPTER ELEVEN: Tournaments, Big Tournaments, and "Un-Tournaments…"

"Gentlemen! Welcome! You honor our Island…" – Speech of the evil Mr. Han, from "Enter the Dragon"

The 60's and 70's are remembered by long-time martial artists as the "Golden Age" of tournament competition. All the famous "names" came – Chuck Norris, Mike Stone, Joe Lewis – Even Bruce Lee. Everybody came! There were matches and breaking competitions, and demonstrations… People from all around – all over the country came – to "make their name" on the tournament circuit. You could see all those faces from magazines like Black Belt and Karate Illustrated, all there! And you could talk to them if you wanted to – "rub shoulders" with everybody and feel good…   It was a real "happening," as we used to say…

…And that was my time. The tournament craze was sweeping the nation, rather like surfing or hula-hoops, and that's when I did most of my competitions.

But tournaments were always popular, even long after I retired from competition. Sid Campbell and I decided to get in on it, too – get in on the craze and hopefully do a good event and make some money, too. We started promoting tournaments at the Oakland Auditorium.

Eventually, we got really GOOD at putting these events on; and ultimately, we did the World Martial Arts Expo together, in 1980.

We put it on in the Oakland Coliseum, and it drew 14,000 spectators. As you can imagine, that was a BIG event –even spectacular. Here's what we did:

At the appointed hour, someone on the public address system, said in a grand voice, "LADIES AND GENTLEMEN: LET THE TOURNAMENT BEGIN!"

And as the echoes of the voice died away, a runner, bearing a torch, just like the Olympics came running forward and lit a flame signaling the beginning of the event.

The mayor of Oakland was a guest, and so was the California Secretary of State March Fong Eu, Ed Parker and Shieh Kien

> "Eric? I don't think that there's anything I wouldn't do for him. He's one of the most REAL, most sincere people I've ever met.
>
> "To give you some idea, I'd just received a promotion and there was apparently some jealousy from some people surrounding that; and the word was that if I showed up at a particular event that was being held in Las Vegas, I'd better have bodyguards. Well, I'd already planned to go there, in-between some seminars I was doing in San Diego, and I wasn't about to change my plans… So I booked a flight to the event, and went.
>
> …And when I got there, I heard, "Hey, Robert!" – and it was Eric. He'd caught wind of what was up, dropped everything, got in his car and drove all the way to Las Vegas – not to be "tough" or aggressive, but just to send the message loud and clear, that if push came to shove, he had my back. Well, thankfully, nobody had anything to say, and I've never had a problem since… and when I went back to San Diego to finish my seminars, Eric was there – he had come to the seminar to support me, _all in the same weekend_. I will NEVER forget that!"   -Robert Suttles, Kajukenbo Grandmaster

– whom you all know as the evil "bad guy" from "Enter the Dragon" – were guests as well... The Beijing Wushu Team was there too; and there were also a number of other martial arts celebrities like Bow Sim Mark... And last but not least, there were lion dancers and lion drums, and many groups performing on stage...

That was one BIG event! We pulled out all the stops.

South Carolina's Keith Vitali eventually fought through the eliminations and won the grand championship.

When attending, it's natural to take events like this for granted... But just to let you know how much work is involved, it took 9 months of planning and 50 people to put it all together.

Now THAT was how to put on a tournament!

But truthfully, tournaments were a LOT of work, and there were always unexpected difficulties and conflicts – the action can be very fast, and the judge might not see a point that had been scored, or he might think he saw a point that had not been scored, or the two competitors might strike at virtually the same instant, to the point that it could be impossible to determine who had scored first... and the competitors and their teachers would argue and get upset...

Even if things go smoothly, and the level of sportsmanship is high, organizing one of those events takes time, planning and effort, and there are always unforeseen problems... Emotions run high, the competition is hot and heavy, and people get really caught-up... So it can be a real pain to put – lots of drama, problems, and stress: Who needs that?!

Sid and I got to talking about this, and instead of complaining endlessly, we came up with an idea. A novel idea. A radical idea: Why not an "un-tournament"? That wasn't a word that we used at the time, of course, but that was certainly the idea:

Martial artists are used to getting notices for tournaments and participating: Why shouldn't it work the same way for something other than a tournament? Well? We already had the know-how to organize an event, and we had the contact list...

We figured, why not? Nothing ventured, nothing gained. There was no reason why martial artists couldn't get together and eat, rather than fight – And it just so happened that I had grandfather's restaurant at my disposal, so the food angle was all taken care of... And I've yet to meet a martial artist that doesn't love to eat...

So we gave it a shot! And it worked!

We called it the "Martial Arts Luau." And I'm pleased to tell you that it was a big hit!

There was food and hula dancing, and for once all the martial artists were in a good mood! No arguing about points, or who got a "by," or who got to fight whom... What a relief! They hugged and enjoyed themselves, and had a great time. It was a lot less trouble, and of course, it was also good for the restaurant, because we made the food!

Actually it was fun making all that food. But one time, long before the movie, "Rocky, with Sylvester Stalone's character hitting the beef ribs in the movie, I have to confess, I decided to "tenderize" a few barbeque pigs ribs by striking them.

That's how I know why Stalone used beef ribs instead: I hit a little too hard and the ribs and spinal cord broke and the meat fell into the fire. So that rack of ribs was history: Oops.

We had a drink that was the specialty of the Luau that we called "Jaws" - after the famous shark movie, – and our joke was that it was on special – and if the customer ordered another, he was brought a different drink from the one he had before. Well, naturally he'd ask why, and we'd tell him that each time the drink was different! That's why it was special!

I'm still not done with terrible jokes like that, or with events like this. I enjoy them, and it's still a good idea. They encourage people to meet others on an even footing, and make new friends and contacts. So they're fun, and serve a useful purpose.

Recently I hosted a monthly "Birthday in the Park" at Warner Park, in front of the Marriott Hotel in Woodland Hills. And the idea was that for anybody who was born in that month, we would celebrate their birthday – Instant party!

It was a natural. When you get right down to it, it's an event, like a tournament. And truthfully, it's easier to organize, and you never know who's going to show up!

For example, I met British rocker Eric Burdon, of "The Animals," and "War," there – you might not know the name, but I'll bet you know his voice from famous hits like "The House of the Rising Sun."

Eric just heard about the event and I guess it was his birthday, so he showed up! So when you put on something like that, you never know who's going to decide to go.

Meanwhile, when I wasn't doing stuff like that, I was on the road just about everywhere, sweeping events across the country. I was undefeated – really on a roll, in those days.

Some sports writer dubbed me the "Little King of Kata" and the name stuck... Here it is half a century later, and people are still calling me that. And truthfully, while there are plenty of truly great kata men out there, nobody ever broke my undefeated record as a forms competitor – especially taking place as it did in the "Golden Age" of competition.

So that's something I can feel good about.

I'm credited with winning more national and international awards than any other martial artist in the United States. Everywhere I'd go, people would say "Eric, do a kata!" I did. Sometimes, we'd even have music, and exotic equipment like Fog machines and strobe lights, music for demonstrations...

It's showy, true, and it may enhance the experience for the audience, but actually, I have mixed feelings about it – it's showy, true, but it also gets away from the real, traditional Zen essence of the martial arts: One person all by himself, moving and training in silence – one with the art, one with nature...timeless – Existing forever in that moment.

All in all, I did, ummm... 44 magazine covers, I think – Black Belt, Karate, Inside Kung Fu, all kinds of magazines... And that's just the ones in the States! I have no idea how many there were in China or Europe. I had a lot of publicity, and many doors opened for me.

I did hundreds of martial arts seminars all around the country that were so well received. I'm still doing them today! Including seminars and regular classes, I've taught over 10,000 people... That's a lot of people.

I even did seminars in Europe - Switzerland and Germany, and some people wanted me to move to Germany to head some schools, but Germany's pretty cold – I don't handle the cold climates as well as I do hot ones, and I didn't speak German, so I declined.

Eventually, they got in touch with Sifu Al, and he decided to go. He wound up doing very well in Germany – he had more than 10,000 students there, so that worked out well for him.

In 1974, I went to Mexico City and did some demonstrations of form, weapons, and self-defense, which was promoted as "American Champion comes to Mexico".

...And the people down there wanted me to open a chain of kung fu schools – Which might have been good, but the air down there at the time was just WAY too polluted. It was so bad that I actually became sick from it, which is unusual for me.

Health has always been the number one priority for me, and I decided that if you can't breathe, you can't live, and you SURE can't train hard, so I said no to the project.

I was getting a lot of notoriety those days, and I started getting calls to appear on various game shows and a lot of talk shows also. Thankfully, I had an agent for films and TV, a fellow named Guy Lee, who worked for the Bessie Loo Agency, who could help me out.

On the "The Price is Right," with Bob Barker, I won – you'll never guess – four huge boxes of baby diapers… Great, what do you do with baby diapers if you're single? At the time I didn't even know any couples with babies, so I donated them to charity.

I did my whip chain set to music for "The Gong Show," with Chuck Barris and Jaye P. Morgan. How did it go? Well, I didn't get gonged!

I also did "Let's Make a Deal," with my friend, Eva. I knew Eva from the tournament circuit, she's a skilled - 6th dan black belt in Kajukenbo, and dancer. She's at home when she performs, just like me. We did the show together and she designed and made costumes for us in only 24 hours. I sent her a big dance dragon, to say thanks - I shipped it all the way from Chinatown, L.A. to Hawaii – I'm told it was the first one in Maui.

On the tournament circuit, I traveled with Bill Wallace and Howard Jackson – we did open tournaments together. I did form and weapons all over.

Eventually, I had been everywhere, all over the country, and proved myself, I felt, to the point that there was nothing left to prove - I figured I had already won everything on the martial arts tournament scene – been there, done that, got the T-shirt, as they say. So in 1973, I decided to retire from competition undefeated. It's good to go out on top.

The second-to-last tournament I competed in was on July 20th, 1973, Korean Taekwondo master Joon Rhee's tournament in Las Vegas, Nevada. It was there that I met karate champion Mike Stone and Priscilla Presley.

Sadly, it was the same day that we got the news that Bruce Lee had died. When we heard what had happened, we all stopped the tournament and everybody had a moment of silence for him.

Bruce, gone... Nobody could believe it. It was a great loss for all of us.

My very last tournament competition was in October, 1973 at the Long Beach Internationals. Joe Lewis fought Steve Sanders for the grand championship and won the fighting division, and I won the grand championship in Kata. So I retired undefeated.

The promoter of that tournament had made a deal with a local car dealership – the idea was that a nice, new, white Lincoln Continental was supposed to be the grand champion trophy, but not enough people showed up for the event to pay for the car, and so, much to everyone's dismay, the dealer drove away with the trophy. Well, that was a disappointment, and we had to take things to court to get everything straightened out. Eventually, I got 80% of the winnings, and 20% went to the lawyers... But that was better than nothing.

I suppose in retrospect, it was a good time to move on...

Looking back at all, my competition and tournament promotion, and movie-making days were pretty active... Sid and I co-promoted the Martial Arts EXPO and the World Tournament, I received Black Belt Magazine and Martial Arts Hall of Fame honors 25 separate times – which might be a record, I honestly don't know.

I was undefeated as a forms and weapons champion from 1970 to 1974 – that IS a record.

I was a 2-time recipient of the Martial Arts Lifetime Achievement Award, and 2 Golden Fist Awards for Best Weapons Champion and Best Forms Champion, was a founding co-member of World Blackbelt, along with other notable martial artists such as Chuck Norris and Bob Wall. I was the Las Vegas Legacy Award Winner, I've been awarded 95 Hall of Fame trophies... And I won over 100 world titles, as the undefeated forms and weapons champion from 1970 to 1974.

I received an Armed Forces Appreciation Award, was the innovator and Certificate as a Trainer of the flight attendant anti-terrorist training school "America in Defense," I worked as an actor and fight choreographer in over 80 movies and TV productions, produced a feature motion picture and received a Southern California Motion Picture Council Golden Halo Award; and I authored 3 martial arts instructional books – one on self defense, one on broadsword, and one on three-section staff - and over 40 training videos – and that's just what I can remember right now, off the top of my head. If I really sat down to think about it, I'm sure there is more.

That's not a bad track record for a little guy from a tiny village in China.

And best of all, I've got 40 black belts under me – some of whom I trained from the beginning, and others who came to me from other styles – to carry on the tradition. If I'm the "Little King of Kata," they're the true jewels in my crown.

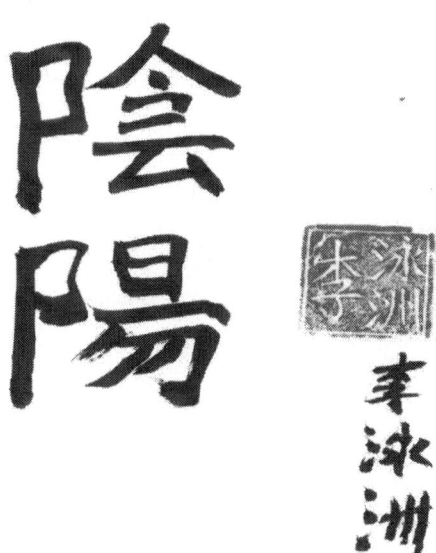

(Yin Yang)

"Yin and Yang, the two principles in nature, and the four seasons are the beginning and the end of everything and they are also the cause of life and death." – Ilza Veith's Translation, The Yellow Emperor's Classic of Internal Medicine.

CHAPTER TWELVE: Hollywood and Making Movies

– *"The more you tell, the more you sell!"*

With all the notoriety I had received from my tournament career, I decided to take a shot at breaking into the movies.

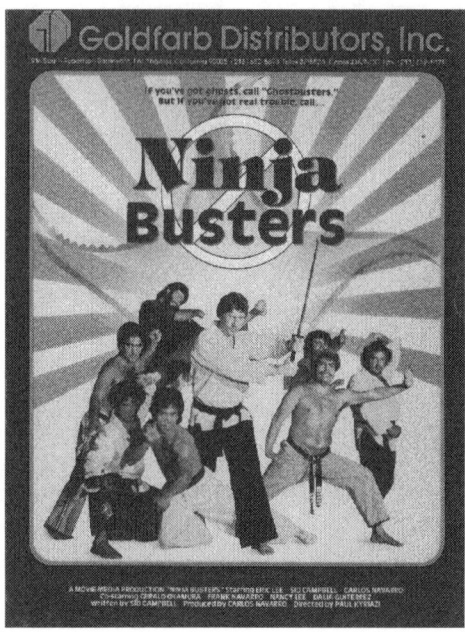

Sid Campbell and I did a movie called "Ninja Buster" with Gerald Okamura – and that was my first real movie role. I played the lead – a character named "Bernie." I don't recommend that people see it... It's not my favorite movie – truthfully, it's not a very good movie at all. "Weapons of Death" is much better... But it was a start for me.

I moved to Los Angeles in late 1976 to be able to explore the idea of getting into films. I was living in an apartment on Argyle, for $95 a month, plus utilities. I was always a big movie fan, as you've seen, and at the time, of course, I was well known, so I felt that I could break into movies.

Everybody has their favorite actors, and favorite movies and so do I. I like action movies - My favorites are "Tombstone," with Kurt Russell, "The Outlaw Josey Wales," with Clint Eastwood, "Enter the Dragon," with Bruce Lee, "The Good, the Bad, and the Ugly," with Clint Eastwood and Eli Wallach – another great actor, "Gladiator," with Russell Crowe, and Jackie Chan's "Drunken Master 2," a Hong Kong movie, and a great comedy performance by Jackie.

Eric & Jackie Chan

My favorite actor is Jackie Chan, for his genius at physical comedy. He's number 1 in my book.

I have to confess, I love jokes and comedy... which is why I like Jackie's work so much. Even corny jokes like "Why don't they have telephone books in China? Because there are too many "Wings and "Wongs," and if they're not careful, they can Wing the Wong number.

Ok, ok, I can hear you groaning out there. I can't help it, I actually LIKE terrible jokes like that. I've memorized hundreds of them to torture people with. What can I say, nobody's perfect... Comedians like Groucho Marx, Charlie Chaplin, the Three Stooges, and Rodney Dangerfield are all aces with me – I love them. I'm a complete fan of comedy and funny accents. I love to tease my friend James Hong – you know him from movies like Blade Runner, and literally dozens of others – by imitating his distinctive high voice with its Chinese accent.

Bruce Lee and Clint Eastwood are tied at the Number 2 slot for me, as far as actors go – Clint was a master of the "tough guy" role: The "Man with No Name," "Dirty Harry," "Philo Beddoe," and "Josey Wales" – nobody can top him for those kinds of roles. And Bruce, of course, was unique. He was the first Chinese to make the big breakthrough from Hong Kong to Hollywood. It's a shame he didn't live longer, he could really have made a huge contribution to the martial arts genre – even bigger than the legacy he left behind. I also like Mel Gibson – he's a talented actor and he selects his roles well, and his action sequences are first rate, so he's my number 3 favorite.

I was offered a lead role in the movie "Death Machine," a non-union movie, but instead I took a small role as a martial artist in "The Killer Elite," which was a union movie filmed down in San Mateo. I thought that was a wiser choice for me, and I believe today that I made the right choice, even though it wasn't a lead role.

I auditioned for "The Killer Elite" in front of famed director Sam Peckinpah. He was the director, and a Hollywood legend who had made movie classics like "The Wild Bunch" and "the Getaway," with Steve McQueen.

His stunt coordinator, Rick Alemany, knew my background, and recommended me for a part, but seeing is believing, so I had to audition for Sam in order to establish myself.

Sam was known as a real "Wildman" on the set – some people have said that his real life exploits on his movie sets were often even wilder than his movies. His exploits were legendary – or perhaps a better word might be "notorious" – in Hollywood…

He was nice to me though. I was hired for two parts – I played a ninja, so my face was covered – which worked well for me because I "double-dipped" with a role as a gangster at the airport also.

I worked on that movie with James Caan, Robert Duvall, and Bo Hopkins; and one of my acting teachers, Mako, was in it too – You know him as the gravel-voiced narrator and little wizard from Conan the Barbarian.

Japanese karate master Takayuki Kubota was there – he was James Caan's teacher at the time… Kali and JKD great Dan Inosanto, Gerald Okamura, Wing Chun man George Cheung, and Eagle Claw stylist Gini Lau, all had parts as well; so in a way, it really was a "Killer Elite" – just without the killing. It was a great film for the martial arts people.

Stirling Silliphant wrote it. I met him and his wife Tianna on that set, and they both became my students. Stirling was a truly great writer – he wrote the iconic "Route 66" Television show starring Martin Milner and George Maharis, about two guys who were off to discover the "real" America in a classic 1962 Corvette convertible; and also the powerful, epic movie, "In the Heat of the Night" with Sidney Poitier and Rod Steiger.

A young, black homicide detective from New York City gets caught up by circumstances, in a murder mystery in the Deep South of the 1960s. Unwillingly teamed up with an isolated white sheriff, the two unlikely allies confront their own prejudices and the deep-seated hostilities of a segregated southern society of that era, as they follow the trail of an unknown killer. If you haven't seen it, it's well worth the effort.

Stirling was a deep thinker and a powerful writer. He had also studied with Bruce Lee, and he co-wrote "The Silent Flute," with Bruce. That movie was to be Bruce's signature showpiece on the essence of martial arts, but sadly, Bruce passed away before the movie could be made. What a movie that could have been with him writing the scenes and Bruce playing an array of dynamic, multiple parts! So the world lost out on that one.

It was eventually made into a movie called, "Circle of Iron," but it was a pale shadow of the smash blockbuster that it would have been with those two powerhouses calling the shots.

Since then, I've done parts in movies like "Big Trouble in Little China," with Kurt Russell, "Rambo II," with Sylvester Stallone, a Bond movie with Timothy Dalton... "The Big Brawl," with Jackie Chan... I was the "axe champion" in "Fist of Iron. In Ring of Fire, and Ring of Fire II, I played Kwong, and I played the lead character in Weapons of Death, and Tong Lee in "Master Demon," which I also produced...

Now that I think back, I've done a LOT of movie roles, some small, some bigger... Let's see, there was "Showdown in Little Tokyo," "Big Trouble in Little China," "Amazing Grace," "Dragon to Dragon," "The Last Dragon Remix," "Assassin X," "Sci-Fighter," "Redemption," "The Education of a Vampire," "The Accidental Spy," "Broken Vessels," "Carjack," "Sworn to Justice," "Tiger Claws II," "Misfit Patrol," "Bloodsport 2," "Fists of Iron," "Death match," "Ring of Fire" and "Ring of Fire II: Blood and Steel," The TV series "Bob", "Talons of the Eagle," "The Master Demon," "In Living Color," "Future Kick," "The Game," The "Separated" episode in the TV series "Vietnam War Story," "Steele Justice," "The Night Stalker", "J.O.E. and the Colonel" – which was a TV movie, "Into the Night," " Ninja Busters," The "Daddy's gone a-Hunting" episode from the TV series "Airwolf," "Going Berserk," "Thirty Seconds Over Little Tokyo" from the TV series "The Greatest American Hero," a made-for-TV movie called "Cocaine and Blue Eyes," "Seven Keys to Singapore" from the TV series "Bring 'Em Back Alive", "Falcon Claw," "The Shinobi Ninja," "Weapons of Death," "Americathon," "Death Machines," "The Jody Affair" from the TV series "Family Affair," "My Name is Manolete," from the "Mod Squad" TV series...

Whew, and that's only a partial list...

Today I've done more than 120 film parts, and I also taught a class at UCLA on movie stunt fighting. There's actually a lot to it - camera angles, how to react, the timing, how NOT to get people hurt... As a good teacher you want your student to be good... that reflects on your teaching.

...I also have a little more than 30 or so credits as a stunt man, a fight scene choreographer, a producer, a writer, a crew member, and have done cameo appearances... I've been the "good guy," the "bad guy," a comedian... I have more than 50 credits as a voiceover artist.

> "Eric's a lover of life: He really studies it. He loves to share philosophy, and he always inspires me – he's got boundless energy and he never has a bad word to say about anybody. So I aspire to that."
>
> –George Snodgrass, martial arts instructor.

So you see I've been around "The Business" a bit.

In Hollywood, above all, the studios wanted dependability – professionalism – They want somebody that will BE there. As they say, "time is money." And it is. The big actors can maybe get away with being temperamental, making demands on set, and arriving late... but soon they get a bad reputation, and nobody will want to work with them.

And the little guys? Well, there's always someone else that can do the part, who will show up on time, and be dependable.

Once in a while, though the "little guys" do have their day, too. It's rare, but it has happened:

I heard a funny story about one of the people I worked with while doing stunts on the movie "Uncommon Valor" - Martial artist and actor, Randall "Tex" Cobb.

At the time, Randall was a tough boxer with a granite jaw and tremendous power – a true "contender" for boxing's heavyweight crown. As a matter of fact, he went on to "go the distance" with champion Larry Holmes, in a title match for Heavyweight Championship of the World.

But this is a story of Randall as an actor... Randall had been hired as the "heavy" in the movie, "The Champ" – playing boxer Roland Bowers, who opposes former champion Billy Flynn (played by veteran actor Jon Voight), who wants one last shot at a comeback.

The movie's climax is an iconic scene where Bowers and Flynn fight a brutal, all-out "war" in the ring. The scenes were difficult and technical, and they required all of Randall's boxing skills to "sell" the action – make it believable, choreograph the scenes, and make John Voight look like a stone pro boxer.

Well, Randall had never acted before, and at the time, he really didn't care about a career in acting – he was dead set on being Heavyweight Champion of the World.

But suddenly, sight-unseen, there he was, immersed in the unfamiliar world of petty Hollywood politics and pecking-orders – a "low-man on the totem pole," and saddled with a schedule to match that rank... despite the fact that he had the responsibility of crafting and choreographing... AND being the stuntman and supporting actor for the most critical scene in the entire movie – the iconic ring "war" between Roland Bowers and former champion Billy Flynn.

So Randall would be called on the set early in the morning and often didn't actually shoot his scenes until late in the afternoon... And there was a small-framed assistant director on the shoot, named "Dave," who seemed to take particularly sadistic delight in ordering the huge boxer around – along with everyone else, of course.

Well, Randall is usually an easy-going kind of guy, but this sort of reception seemed disrespectful to him; and he silently chaffed under the treatment, quietly biding his time, waiting for justice to prevail.

Finally, late in the shoot with tens of thousands of dollars of film "in the can," as they say, it was time for Randall to make a statement about respect...

So suddenly, there in the middle of shooting some of the most crucial scenes in the film, Randall started missing his call time, showing up later... and later... and later...

So there they all were: If you can picture it, the scene would be all ready to shoot – all the actors, crew, camera men, lighting and sound technicians, directors – were in position, all set, all ready to go...

...And everybody'd be standing around going, "Ummm, where's Randall?"

Well, as you can imagine, this all gets expensive fast, when the clock is ticking and all of these people are being paid.

There's a saying on movie sets that goes: If you're early, you're on time. If you're on time, you're late. If you're late, you're fired – And normally, that's a true saying...

...Except, at that point Randall was literally irreplaceable: Nobody else could do the part, and since he and Jon Voight were the only actors in the scene, it wasn't like you could "shoot around" him. And on sets, there are always crucial things like "running over-budget," and "running way behind schedule," to consider... So it was fair to say that sheer panic set in.

Finally, in desperation, "Dave" was dispatched to explain these things to Randall, see what the problem was, and ask him – humbly, for once – if there was anything he could do to help.

Well, this was EXACTLY the opportunity that Randall had been waiting for: At long last, his moment had arrived!

So Randall grinned his biggest, best, Texas smile at "Dave," and explained patiently,

> "There's nothing you can do, Dave... There's **_NOTHING_** you can do: You see, for weeks you've been getting me

up at the crack of dawn for absolutely no reason on God's green earth, and making me sit around the set all day long, like a bump on a log, doing nothing but looking stupid; and I put up with that...

"Meanwhile, you get to yell at everybody, order people around, and carry on as if you were God's little gift to Hollywood, and just make life generally miserable for everybody and their dog, here on the set.

"Well I want you to KNOW, Dave, that I put up with all that for a REASON. And the REASON I put up with all this nonsense, was because I KNEW that the day would come that you'd have too much film and too much money invested in me to FIRE me... And TODAY'S the DAY, Dave!

"You see, I'm not really an actor, it's not what I do, I don't care about it one way or another – I'm a boxer, and you may not think much of that, but that's what I am and I'm proud of it. And the plain truth is that since I'm NOT an actor, I don't give a damn about your schedule, OR Hollywood... And for that matter, I honestly don't care whether I ever act in LIFE again... So you can't intimidate me, and you can't FIRE me..."

...For added emphasis, Randall stood up, rising to his full 6 feet, 3 inches of carved heavyweight contender, and towered meaningfully over the diminutive little assistant director, looking down at him with his hands on his hips...

"And as a matter of fact... You can't even HIT me, now, can you, Dave?!"

Well, needless to say, "Dave" lost that exchange... Which in the Hollywood world is kind of a "big deal," because Dave was an "assistant director" – and assistant directors have a LOT of power on a movie set. Basically their word is LAW. So nothing even REMOTELY like this had ever happened to Dave before, and he was simply gob-smacked – he just couldn't quite believe what had just happened...

So for the rest of the day, "Dave" wandered around the set in a sort of daze, telling anybody who'd listen, "And THEN he said..."

I guess you could say that "Dave" really got what was coming to him, that day. :)

Well, that story made Randall quite the hero to all the "little guys" on the set who dream about doing something like that...

They'll tell you, "you'll never work in this town again," if you pull such a stunt – but you can take one look at Randall's LONG list of screen credits that followed "The Champ," and see how much that claim is worth.

Events like that are rare in "the Biz," though. I certainly never got to "rock the boat" like that; and thankfully, unlike Randall, I never a had reason to. I was treated well, and I was Mr. Dependable. They'd call me up and say, "Mr. Lee, we're shooting in such and such a place on such and such a day: Can you make it?"

There's only one answer for that: "Yes, I can!" And then you have to BE there, on time, every time. You have to be 100% dependable, because they can always call someone else.

And I have to say that in my case, dependability paid off. I've been fortunate: Unlike most actors, I was able to work regularly. I even did voice-overs for Jackie Chan, but I would always turn down the stereotypical roles that Hollywood offered – the ones depicting Chinese with the little pig-tails and so forth, because I felt it was a dehumanizing stereotype, and I had a lot of pride.

I wasn't what you'd call a major Hollywood star, of course, but I can't complain – I did a few lead roles and SAG-AFTRA was always very good to me. They protect the actors against fraud, and make sure they get paid, and that they get their residuals – royalties paid to people in the entertainment industry for things like reruns, syndication, DVD release, or online streaming release. I appreciate SAG-AFTRA – they've taken good care of me.

I auditioned a LOT in those days. Each time was like a high school reunion… seeing all the same competition – but I got tired of it. When the studios throw you a bone, it seems like you are all fighting over the bone like a hungry dog.

Since I'm comfortable both in front of and behind the camera, and I understood how to both direct and produce, I decided to liberate myself from all that drama, and do my OWN projects; and I'm continuing to do that today. They're not big projects – not yet anyway, although I'm giving that some thought, too – but my philosophy is, hey, at least I'm doing them.

In Hollywood, you can look down your nose at the little productions and wait literally forever for that big, blockbuster movie role that's going to make you a famous, household name: But my feeling is, why wait and dream about it happening "someday," when you can really DO it on a smaller scale, NOW.

Technology in the movies has evolved by leaps and bounds, and this has opened the doors for small-scale productions. High quality, technical effects, and equipment that used to cost literally millions of dollars is now available for just a fraction of the cost – some cost practically nothing, in fact – so as far as movies go, it's a good time for the "little guy," with low overhead, who can "work smart."

You DO have to have the right team to get the job done. That's crucial. I think perhaps my biggest strength is that I know how to recognize talent and DELEGATE... The skills involved in putting a movie together are so diverse, and so specialized that no one person can even HOPE to do it all himself. It's just not possible. So you have to depend upon others, and the people you depend upon have to be CONSISTENT at making it happen. If you have a good team that has your back, it's amazing what you can accomplish WITHOUT having the backing of a multimillion-dollar production.

It's tough making it in Hollywood. Thousands of actors arrive each year, but only a tiny fraction of them work regularly; and similarly, if you're trying to get started in production, raising money for a project can be very difficult and disheartening.

Once I volunteered my time for a documentary on fight scene choreography – I did it for free because I knew the people making it didn't have money, and I know how difficult it is when film makers are first starting out. Getting the money for those first film projects is tough, when you don't really have a track record – and then you still have to know how to set up the shoots, how to visualize how it's all going to go, and how to set up a week. So I did them a favor. I think it's good for the spirit to do random acts of kindness like that.

Later I received a card from the people who did the documentary that said,

"In all the crumbling sidewalks of Hollywood we can still find beautiful roses"

I was quite touched by that.

ERIC LEE IN "THE LAST ADVENTURE"
Starring: Robert Ramos, Ralph Castellanos, Lanei Lee
Louis Winfield Bailey, Gerald Okamura, Gini Lau, Sid Campbell
Produced by Richard Sydel. Written & Directed by Paul Kyriazi
A Cinamerica Production ©1978 Panavision · Technicolor

Eric Lee, Friend, James Hong

Dan Inosanto with Eric Lee

Eric Lee with a good friend actor/martial artist Jeff Langton

Eric Lee, Al Dacascos, Mike Mather, Mark Gerry

EMPEROR PRODUCTION presents THE MASTER DEMON, an action adventure motion picture starring ERIC LEE, GERALD OKAMURA and KAY BAXTER, with special guest star SID CAMPBELL. Also starring STEVE NAVE and AVA CADELL. Produced by Eric Lee. Co-Produced by Art Camacho. Directed by Art Camacho and Samuel Martin Oldham. Written by Samuel Martin Oldham.

Eric Lee as Tong Lee. **Sid Campbell** as Li Besecker and **Steve Nave** as Cameron in Emperor Production's **The Master Demon**.

Photo credit: Adrian Ibarra

(Honor)

"All the great things are simple, and many can be expressed in single word: freedom, justice, honor, duty, mercy, hope." - Winston Churchill

CHAPTER THIRTEEN: Just a TINY Taste of Superstardom!

– "It's been a hard day's night…" – The Beatles, 1964

The movies were a pretty exciting experience for me, but I did have one experience that was far beyond movie-making, and that was visiting Chile back in 1986. I owe that experience to Kenpo Karate great Ed Parker. We went there with French karate champion Dominic Valeria – Europe's master of the foot sweep, and Okinawan Karate great Tadashi Yamashida.

I enjoyed the trip immensely, but it also gave me a new appreciation for being just an ordinary guy. Why? I'll tell you…

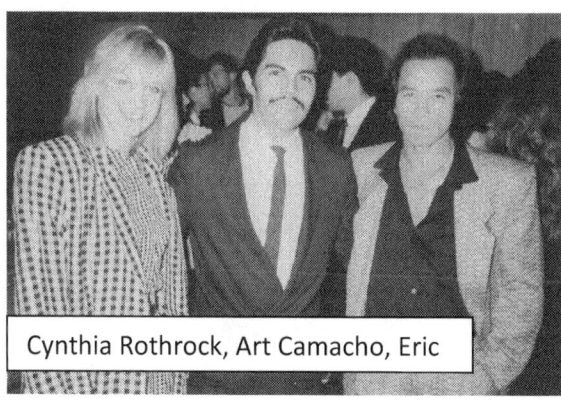
Cynthia Rothrock, Art Camacho, Eric

Early on in our trip, we actually visited the Presidential Palace – We were met by a 5-star general, and he opened a big door, and there was the President of Chile. He welcomed us and we talked with him a bit – it turns out that he was a real martial arts fan. And boy did he roll out the red carpet! As it turned out, he was a real, dyed-in-the-wool, hardcore martial arts aficionado, and he gave us the mother of all welcomes to his country!

Eric Lee with politicians and prime minister of Chile

Julio Hernandez, a student of mine from Puerto Rico – one of my 40 black belts – interpreted for us. Ed Parker's black belt, a fellow named Arturo, was the ONLY guy in the whole country who was formally in charge of administration over ALL the martial arts in Chile – an authority granted to him directly by the President – can you imagine?

And the people! I don't know how the President managed to generate that kind of enthusiasm for us, but wow! We literally could not walk down the street, because of the thousands of welcoming crowds in the street -

To say that the people were hospitable is a HUGE understatement – They took us to restaurants, we went shopping... We were literally treated like kings – And everywhere we went, we were absolutely overwhelmed by the crowds. It was stunning!

There were so many people in the streets – just to see us! And they were literally wild with enthusiasm – I've never seen anything like it before or since. There were so many people in the streets to welcome us that we were late for the expo we were doing.

We went to a TV station there – to do some pre-publicity, before our demo, or perhaps it was a news show – I'm not really sure... I'm at a loss as to why we needed any more excitement generated than we already had – the whole country seemed to be running at a fever pitch... But it was scheduled, and so we did it.

That kind of excitement really is contagious; so all of our energy levels were way, WAY up...

How far up? Well, for example, during his time in front of the cameras, Ed Parker was doing his Kenpo techniques, and his energy level was up so high that when he stamped down on the hardwood stage, it actually broke underneath him: WHACK! His foot actually went right through that hardwood floor. Now that's a lot of energy.

When we finally got to the Expo and did demonstrations, it was ALL brand new to the crowds of people – They were already excited to the max BEFORE our show, and they'd never seen what we did before, so they went absolutely wild. We were treated like superheroes by the people. It was if they believed we could fly – I can't possibly explain the level of energy that they had for us, there's just no words to describe it.

For some reason the stage mic didn't work properly, so the master of ceremonies used a bull horn, and even THAT seemed to dump more fuel on the fire of the crowd's energy...

We did a couple hours' worth of demonstration – and the crowd's reaction was simply incredible. They literally put us on their shoulders and carried us around! Looking back on it now, it's STILL amazing to think about!

It was absolutely unique. Unless you've experienced it for yourself, you literally can't believe people going that crazy over you. It's simply surreal.

Our second Demo was in another part of the country – we flew there, and the crowds there went just as nuts.

It was an amazing experience; one of the most memorable experiences I ever had. I've never experienced anything like it ever again, and I don't imagine that I ever will – it was a once-in-a-lifetime experience – even better than the big receptions I got in Europe!

Still, I'm glad I don't have to live my life like that every day. I can still go to the store or enjoy a movie without being mobbed by fans. That's a luxury that the superstars don't have. Can you visualize what it would be like, not to be able to walk down the street without drawing a huge crowd of people?

People were really so excited that they took parts of our clothes and our shoes for souvenirs. That really happens!!! You hear stories about this, and you think to yourself, "No WAY!" Yes, way. I saw it myself! It really does happen that the crowd gets that crazy.

So thanks to that experience I can relate to what the Beatles must have experienced at the height of "Beatle mania," getting mobbed and running away from wild crowds of hysterical, screaming fans.

I used to listen to all those stories of the Beatles, and I'd think, "Why would they run?" Now I KNOW why, because I experienced it first-hand.

So as a result of that experience it's easy for me to understand all those stories about big stars putting on disguises so they can go out like regular people, and it makes me appreciate being relatively anonymous – something that just about all of us take for granted without so much as a second thought – can be a real treasure.

Still... That has to be, hands down, my absolute best reception EVER. What an experience! I wouldn't trade it for anything, but I'm also glad that I don't have to live my whole life like that. I'm sure it must get old quick.

(Love)

"When you love someone, you love the whole person, just as he or she is, not as you would like them to be." – Leo Tolstoi

CHAPTER FOURTEEN: Kay Baxter

Eric & Kay Baxter

It was shortly after that time -1987 - that I met the woman who would become the love of my life. Her name was Kay, and she was a world-class body builder and a gymnast – one of the best in the country.

We met while I had a job modeling clothes – pants only, no shirt, as it so happened. I was in L.A., at the northwest corner of Sunset and Sepulveda, and my friend Sam Oldham, who was a skilled cameraman, was doing a video for her, and they dropped by my little event. He introduced her to me as a "classy lady," and she certainly was.

We got to talking – she had a very nice, charming personality – She said that she was interested in training in the martial arts, and we seemed to have a lot in common and hit it off right away – so she began training with me.

The people who wrote the bodybuilding magazines called her "The Duchess" – much the same as I was known as the "Little King of Kata," and she was in peak condition - physical in the same way that I was physical. So there was immediate chemistry, as they say. She was a Libra – very balanced with other people and with herself – practical and financially stable, and we got along from the very beginning.

She had her own house in Venice, and one day she invited me over to her place, and she cooked dinner for me... and one thing naturally led to another... And from that time on, we were together.

I had a big house at 23025 Ardwick St. in Woodland Hills at the time, – And Kay eventually got a house around the block. People would come over to party from about 7PM to Midnight, just about every day – there was a swimming pool, a fireplace... it was a perfect place for partying. My friends would be there, and Kay would bring her friends over to mix...

Actually, everybody would come... James Lew, Adriano Emperado... just about everybody in the martial arts showed up there sooner or later. That it was before GPS systems, so the biggest problem was telling people how to get there, and once they got there, where to find the bathroom. We were all young, and it really was great getting together and socializing.

Those were good days!

What can I tell you about Kay? She was like an awakening for me. She liked to do everything I liked to do, and I liked to do everything she liked to do. She brought out the best in me, and I brought out the best in her – two as one, like the soul mates you read about in books. She lit up my life.

To this day, she was the closest woman in my life. And there was nothing in the world that I would have wanted more, than to spend the rest of my life with her…

…But sadly, it was not to be – She was killed in an automobile accident in 1988, when her Corvette rolled over on Mulholland Drive.

"I'm a martial artist and a doctor of acupuncture and Chinese medicine. Eric and I met way back when we were auditioning for movies and he was kind enough to give me a ride home. We happened to run into each other after he lost Kay, and he mentioned he was depressed about it, and the way he talked I thought it had happened just a matter of months ago, but it turned out it was 4 years before, and I was like "Wow, you're still depressed? What can I do to get you out of it?

"Well, I realized that Eric needed some real help to be able to move on, so I had him stay at my place, and I'd treat him with acupuncture, sometimes twice a day, and we'd do Tai Chi and Chi Gung together in the mornings… I made meals, everything… Well, after about a month he started feeling better, and was able to move ahead with his life."

-Dr. Rick Lengyel, Acupuncturist and practitioner of Chinese Medicine; United States Army Special Forces Medic, Retired, Vietnam veteran.

She was my one true love. And suddenly she was gone. It was like the sun had suddenly gone out.

It was devastating for me. I simply couldn't cope with that loss. There is no worse thing than losing somebody you love – for once in my life, I didn't have enough coping skills to deal with something like that – Her loss was more devastating to me than anything else in my life. I honestly didn't know how to get over it.

Life has to go on, people say, but that loss... I was down for years, really, and it took a lot of help from my friends to move on with my life, because for the first and only time in my life, I really couldn't cope, couldn't move on.

I owe a lot to my friends, for helping me get through that difficult time – and especially to my friend, Dr. Rick Lengyel, an acupuncturist and fellow black belt, who realized how depressed I truly was, and gave me a lot of support and encouragement.

I wasn't getting out, I wasn't going places, I wasn't doing anything...Life had lost its meaning. The things I used to take such an interest in suddenly didn't seem to matter anymore.

Well Dr. Rick realized what I was going through – I guess he had the background and training to know, and he was a friend enough to realize that somebody actually needed to intervene on my behalf, to help me out of it. He was actually kind enough to take me into his own home for a month. I had a room to myself there, and he knew how to keep an eye on me, and he showed me how to lead myself out of that sad, isolated place I was in. So I'm grateful for his kindness and support – otherwise, I really might never have bounced back.

True friends are a blessing. They're like family, except that while you can choose your friends, you can't choose your family. I owe a lot to Dr. Rick.

Eric Lee, Chuck Norris, Dr. Rick Langyel

Today, I still date women, but I have no steady relationship. Maybe there will be one, someday… maybe not. Time will tell.

(Health)

"It is health that is real wealth and not pieces of gold and silver." – Mahatma Gandhi

CHAPTER FIFTEEN: I Return to China

   – *"You can't go home again." – Thomas Wolfe*

   – *"I did." – Eric Lee*

In 2005, I took a break from everything I'd been doing to host my China Tour. What could be more natural!?

Being Chinese, I certainly knew China, and I spoke the language and knew all the customs. I was already adept at planning events from my tournament days, and Chinese tourism was booming at the time, so it really was a great idea, and I was ideally suited for it. I like people, I like to host, and it makes people happy... And that makes ME happy. So I did it!

I put that idea together and did that for five years, until 2010. Some of the people went 3 or 4 times with me, so I guess they really enjoyed themselves. People still call me wanting to know when the next one is, but I have to tell them I'm not doing that right now.

The first year I went with a co-host, actress and martial artist, and my personal friend, Cynthia Rothrock. Cynthia has done a lot of Hong Kong movies, so she had that experience to draw upon.

Eric Lee & Cynthia Rothrock

We were the hosts, but of course we also had a separate tour guide, a specialist, who knows how to handle all the little details like visas, and scheduling for 10 days, so that we had all the bases covered, and everybody knew each day what they were going to do.

Ten days seems to be about the ideal length of time for a tour of that kind. I'm used to that kind of traveling, of course, but I've found that for many people – especially for people over 55 - any longer than that is a bit too much, but ten days is just right.

It was a custom tour, and we visited many places - Beijing, the Great Wall of China, Chengdu, Shanghai... We visited a silk factory, attended a tea ceremony, drove around on a tour bus, and were treated to Chinese massages and a Wu Shu demo, went shopping and saw the sights... There were lots of things to do there, and we enjoyed them all.

The tour included three meals a day and booking in a 4 or 5 star hotel. It was a custom tour and the cost at the time ran from $2,000 to $3,500 a piece – which was pretty fair, I think, considering that we went all the way to China.

One year we also visited Hawaii, and Sifu Al Dacascos was there to share the "aloha spirit" with everyone. For those of you who don't know, the "aloha spirit" is our awareness of being a part of all, and all being a part of us. When others have pain - it is also our pain. When there is joy - it is also our joy. It's fellowship, humanity... belonging. The kind of friendship and good feeling divides our sorrows and doubles our blessings in life.

Many of the people who went with us on these tours were martial artists, and for martial artists like Sifu Al and me, our students are an extension of our "chi" – our energy, our life-force. So in a way, we are family, and we have a special bond with them.

> *"Eric creates, inspires, and fuels ideas that become a reality, through his laser-focused passionate drive and follow through. Who else could decide to become a singer and just start recording CD's? I jump on his bandwagon to pursue positive adventures in life. Many, many people have ideas but they don't follow through on them like he does. "*
>
> - *Joycelyne Lew, actress, magician, comedienne, burlesque dancer, and entertainer, with a master's degree in Education – "Kem" in the hit TV series, "Kung-Fu"*

They all trusted me to take good care of them, and I did. Everybody had a great time. The tour ran amazingly smooth. In five years there were no real emergencies or crises. The only trouble that we ever had was that one person had a little stomach pain, which was quickly remedied – that was it!

Joycelyne Lew

Some of the martial artists with us on the tour got to train at Shaolin Temple, which was a real treat for them.

For more than a thousand years, and to this very day, it is still a center where the martial arts are taught - There are some 1,500 kids up to age 10 or 12 who train every day at the temple. Rising at 5AM. Training there is very strict. They're taught to respect, and not talk back. In addition to all the techniques, there are plenty of horse stances and pushups to make the body very strong, and some of the monks there can perform remarkable feats of skill and martial prowess.

Oddly enough there's a Korean Taekwondo center right next to Shaolin Temple – the monks and the Taekwondo practitioners all get along fine.

The Shaolin Temple has a deep place in the heart of every martial artist, because it is the legendary birthplace of the martial arts in

China and has endured through the centuries – it burned three separate times, but always seems to rise again.

Everybody has seen the TV series "Kung Fu," which features scenes at the Temple from the hero's days of training there as a boy.

All kinds of legends and stories exist about it, both old and new, and many different versions …each one is the "true" and "authentic" one, of course.

Perhaps you've heard some yourself? I think that the important thing is that there are stories, just like there are stories in the West about Merlin, and Excalibur, and King Arthur and his knights; and that people still tell them.

Legends are like that! People come and go, but legends live forever, and the people who once lived those stories pass from this brief mortal life, into myth… The stories are told and re-told… And the legend grows and grows with each re-telling…

> …One version of the Shaolin story goes that an Indian sage named "Bodhidharma," whom we Chinese call "Damo," made the long and dangerous trek from India to China, bringing with him the knowledge of the martial arts, and also the discipline of Chan meditation.
>
> Eventually, he settled at the Shaolin Temple, there in Henan. Seeing that the monks were kind and good hearted, but in poor condition, he began training them to restore their health, strengthen their spiritual skills,

and give them a means to defend themselves from bandits and wild beasts.

To this day, one can see the great training hall where the monks once trained. The places in the brick floor where they each stood to train, and stamped the ground during their formal exercises, are deeply indented from the power of their movements over centuries. Ancient frescoes still adorn the walls, showing the monks training.

Monks are said to prize peace above all – but one time, they made an exception, and that one time turned out to be a big mistake:

The story – or at least this version of it – goes that the land was at risk from some threat – a rebellion, an invasion... some war or other.

Having heard of the monks' reputations as fierce fighters, someone, a general, the emperor... someone powerful... put out a desperate call for help.

At long last, despising war, but fearing for the safety of the people, the monks decided that they had to help. So they took up arms, joined the battle, and defeated the enemy. Order was restored, and the land was once again at peace.

However...

Seeing the incredible skill of the monks, the soldiers who fought alongside them were absolutely terrified of their abilities. And so these stories filtered back to the soldiers' leader, who was also amazed by the tales of the seemingly invincible monks with their remarkable skills, who had turned the tide of battle and allowed the army to triumph against seemingly insurmountable odds.

Over the years, the leader, enjoying the fruits of his great victory, became more and more powerful, and more and more wealthy... And eventually, as his power grew, and grew; and he became jaded and corrupt, as men with too much power often do. As the old saying goes, power tends to corrupt, and absolute power tends to corrupt absolutely.

So while the leader gained more and more wealth and power, he also became more and more distant from the people; and grew more and more indifferent to their hopes, dreams... and eventually, even to their most basic needs.

He no longer believed that his rule existed to provide the people with freedom and prosperity. He believed that they existed to give him power and position. And so the people suffered, and so did the land.

But even with the leader's great wealth and power, lingering stories about those loyal but deadly monks, bothered him deeply, because he knew that they were still there... And he realized, deep in his corrupt heart, that if these monks ever rose up against him, he didn't stand a chance.

This thought troubled him... It is said that thoughts have power, and time has weight – one can see its effects upon all things. And over time, in this corrupt leader's mind, those thoughts became fears, and those fears grew... and grew...

And so, despite all he had, he became afraid, and insecure, and filled with anger. The skills of those deadly monks and the thought of them rising up against him with all their skills, haunted his thoughts and even dreams, and eventually left him with no peace.

So at long last he decided that he would have to remove this threat, by eliminating his former allies forever.

…But Shaolin was like a great fortress, and between that, and the awesome fighting skills of the monks, the idea of defeating them seemed an impossible problem… Other means would have to be employed… Perhaps treachery would prove a more effective tool than mere military might.

So the leader began plotting and scheming… Eventually, through spies and operatives he had sent out, a traitor was discovered – Perhaps he was someone who had been thrown out of the temple for misdeeds, and was resentful of his former teachers and brother monks… or perhaps he was someone whose greed and the glitter of gold inspired him to betray his teachers and the temple that had been his home…maybe both… Or perhaps there was some other reason that sparked betrayal in his heart… Who knows!

But in any case, the traitor knew the secret ways in and out of the temple, and whatever his motivation might have been, he was eventually induced to betray those secrets.

And so late one night, while all the monks slept, stealthy teams of men were sent out, and a great fire was set, which cut off all escape and burned the temple to the ground.

Only five monks – the most skilled of all the Shaolin monks – somehow survived the great fire. These five, known as the "Five Ancestors," scattered throughout the countryside, and taught their skills to the people. And eventually, utilizing those very skills that they had been taught, the people rose up against the tyranny of their unjust and oppressive ruler… and won their freedom.

Eric & Bruce Lee's Brother: Robert

That's how the story goes. If it isn't true, it ought to be. If you have a better one, you can tell that one instead of this one – It's fine with me! That's what legends are all about, after all!

(Tae Kwon Do)

"Nothing can stop the man with the right mental attitude from achieving his goal; and nothing on earth can help the man with the wrong mental attitude." – Thomas Jefferson

CHAPTER SIXTEEN: Back to the Present!

Do what you love to do.

Talk to people.

So... here we are, back to the present; back to here and now.

Today, I am doing exactly what I want to do, doing what I love... leading the life of an artist... And I'm grateful for that freedom. I consider myself fortunate and well blessed to have lived my life and done as well as I have.

I'm still doing martial arts, of course, and I do my Tai Chi and my forms everyday for health, and to keep my skills sharp and ready... And, in addition to keeping up my martial arts skills, I enjoy walking several miles a day.

I also like to see all the new things that the modern generation of martial artists is doing – there are some amazing acrobatics that I might have learned to pursue as a young man, but at 72 I still like to watch – We have a saying: "Just because you're on a diet, that doesn't mean you can't read the menu."

And truthfully, after more than half a century of training, I feel satisfied that I've got a good handle on understanding and living that discipline, and so for a new challenge, a new experience... to be a beginner, all over again, I'm learning music.

Doing new things and staying interested keeps you young, I believe. It's a new challenge, and I feel it's good for balancing out my emotions and cultivating my health, and, well... I like it.

Knowledge is created by beginning with what you know, to what you don't know, and I like sensation of learning things for the first time. And for me, music is a good transition - Music is performance, entertainment, and of course I'm quite familiar with that, so a lot of the skills transfer, and that gives me an edge to learn quicker.

Actually, I find that music is actually very similar in many ways to martial arts – and especially, I find that Tai Chi and music are complementary skills that have a great deal in common: To be good at either you have to relax and really enjoy it… And I'm looking to the future, as well: I might not always be able to do jump-spinning heel kicks, but I feel I can always sing, so it makes good sense to do something that can still allow me to continue to enjoy the experience of performance.

> "Eric Lee is everything that you would imagine that a sifu/grand master would be. Every day he lives in balance – that means mind/body/spirit. His posture, and every single thing he does is in balance. As a friend he is very conscientious and thoughtful, and… adorable in a lot of ways."
>
> –Sara Matthews, registered dietician/nutritionist, filmmaker, ballet dance, fitness trainer and martial artist

I consider myself an artist, and I'm fortunate to be able to do what I want to do, and live an artistic lifestyle…

Most people concentrate on what they DON'T have. But for health, I like to focus on what I DO have: I like that saying, "Count your blessings." It's a true saying.

But also, all that I do, cultivates health. What you think and feel inside has power – the inside eventually affects the outside, so it pays to cultivate a lifestyle that allows you to relax, get enough exercise, and think good thoughts that make you happy and lead you to doing more, and experiencing the things that you love while you are here – you could call it, "feeling for healing."

Greglon Lee, Jason Lee, Eric, Sid Campbell

For me, learning music is a part of that. I've been doing music for about six years now. It's a good feeling – I think that I've got a pretty good handle on what I'm doing with the martial arts after all the years I've been involved in it, and I love the experience of learning something brand new, and being a true beginner at something again.

At first, I wasn't sure how I was going to approach learning music. Whenever you embark on something new, I've noticed, there is a certain tendency to "re-invent the wheel," so to speak... But that's ok, it's all part of learning.

I bought a variety of different instruments – saxophone, trumpet, keyboard, drums, piano, guitar, even a guzheng - which is a kind of big Chinese zither... A whole bunch of instruments?

They seem to have an energy about them that I enjoy feeling, just by looking at them. Go to a music store sometime, and you'll see what I mean – the soft glow of the brass and silver, and the delicate figure in the polished wood of the stringed instruments... all just waiting to go home with someone and be played... It seems to have a certain magic all its own.

My friend and student, Rodney, a professional pianist and composer who has played with some of the very best – Stevie Wonder, Miles Davis, Freddie Hubbard... – commented when he got a look at all those instruments, that it was going to be interesting to see what I finally settled down with.

I now realize that he was right – It takes a lifetime to master each of these instruments, although for some of the instruments like percussion, woodwinds, and keyboards, there is a lot of "crossover" in how they're played, which makes it possible to master more than one.

I've finally settled on voice, though, mainly because I feel that it's healthy – the breathing and the relaxation that it cultivates are good for you – similar to Tai Chi in a way.

"Chi" is something that you hear a lot about in the Chinese martial arts... It's life energy, intrinsic power. It can also be translated as "air," and it has an intimate association with the breathing. It's like medicine in a way – a little can heal, a lot can kill. Acupuncture, which has been documented scientifically, is based upon adjusting the flow of Chi through the body.

Basically, in Tai Chi, we say that chi flows when you're utterly relaxed – so relaxed that you forget yourself – you lose yourself in the movement, and little by little, you forget the movement, and the movement does you. It's a kind of natural magic, in a way.

Voice is like that: Also, it's natural, we're born with it, there's no instrument to get in the way, and like Tai Chi, it has a great deal to do with the breathing. I feel that it's good for cultivating health, and I enjoy it.

So I'm now developing my "pipes," as the singers say... Friends say that I have a pleasing tenor voice, and that my intonation is good, which is an advantage – things like that can't really be taught, I'm told...

You could say that I'm an older singer, but as you know, I don't really believe in "old," so that's not a barrier for me – Hey, jazz singer Tony Bennett is still doing a fine job at 92, so I've got a ways to go before I catch up to him...

And in any case, a little licorice and cinnamon tea – throat coat – takes good care of those little tickles and scratchiness in the throat that crop up from time to time; and if you bite the tip of your tongue just a little – don't hurt yourself, of course – that produces more saliva to get the throat lubricated a bit better – so there's a little tip for the other aspiring singers out there....

I've always enjoyed music, that's... I'm broadening out now, listening to different styles – popular mostly, but also some jazz and classical, like Schubert's "Ave Maria"... Jazz is still difficult for me – it's a high-level skill, and I don't quite understand it yet, but I'm learning.

I pick songs I listen to – I actually discipline myself to listen to music for several hours each day. YouTube is a wonderful resource for this – They say there's more information there, than is stored in the entire Library of Congress. It's certainly true for music! Just about everybody is literally right at your fingertips: Lady Gaga and Tony Bennett, Elvis, Elton John, Andre Bocelli, Willie Nelson, Sinatra... you name it – anybody, right at your fingertips.

I'm experimenting with writing songs myself – I'm just now doing one about my little dog, Bela. Maybe they're good, maybe not – I don't concern myself much with that: If I feel like doing it, I do it... Other people can decide whether it's good or not – That's not my department.

I like my dog. She's a good friend and great company. Someone once said that a dog was the only love that money can buy, and I believe that's true. She's in one of the music videos that I did, so she's already a star pet. It takes a dog only about seven seconds to let go of a negative experience, and be happy again, and I'm trying to learn that wisdom from her. You really can learn a lot from dogs... So I wrote a song about her: That's freedom... That's what I came to America for, all those years ago.

Music and entertainment are good for your soul, and hopefully others may like it too... But if they don't, who cares – I do it because *I* like it, not to win the approval of others.

I'm also cultivating a few skills on piano and guitar– chords, mostly, so that I can accompany myself if I want to. I started doing music at 67. I've been told that I have a pleasing tenor voice, and a good sense of intonation – which is good, because it's difficult to teach those particular skills. I still have to concentrate to keep my accent out of the notes, because it distracts from the song, but I'm working on it.

From my years of demonstration and competition, and my roles in films, I already know how to perform – how to connect with an audience, so that's a plus.

And I do have one advantage that most musicians don't have – including many accomplished musicians: I know how to produce. So I've got 26 songs that I like, that I'm in the process of recording – I'm going to make a couple music videos – which is a luxury most beginners don't have.

I still consider myself a beginner, but I've always enjoyed performance – which is another advantage: I'm very comfortable in front of the camera and in front of a live audience. And I'm doing this for me – if people like the music, great; if they don't, that's OK too: It's a free country! So all those disciplines complement each other, you see.

Not everybody's got "fire" like me, and I consider it a blessing – I plan on respecting and honoring that blessing by taking full advantage of it.

I still keep up with my art – my paintings and especially my calligraphy has some demand, and I enjoy doing that. I'm currently working on a painting of; believe it or not; the famous gunfight at the OK Corral. I was inspired to do that one by the Kurt Russell movie, "Tombstone." It's currently my favorite movie.

I'm told that as movies go, it was historically VERY accurate, in some cases, *right down to the dialogue that was actually spoken*, as recorded in contemporary accounts, and I was fascinated by it all...

I went there with a couple of friends, and my dog, Bela. I still love to travel and explore new places, and Tombstone is a great example of why:

It's an amazing place. It got its name from a fellow named Ed Schieffelin, who was a scout for the army, back when Arizona was a wild, desolate, and dangerous place. Ed had a habit of going out into the vast desert alone, and prospecting for gold and silver in his spare time.

His friends at Fort Huachuca, feared for his safety, because there were hostile tribes in the area, in addition to the usual rattlesnakes, scorpions, and gila monsters, and the near-total absence of shade and water. Even the sun was merciless, with temperatures at times exceeding 120 degrees in the shade – and there WAS no shade. And because he went out all alone, he had no one to help him if something unexpected happened.

His friends warned him, "Ed, the only 'rock' you will find out there will be your own tombstone."

Sure enough, they were right – in a way. One day, while prospecting in a remote area known as Goose Flats, Ed became one of the rare miners in history to achieve every prospector's dream: Ed "struck it rich." There before his disbelieving eyes was the Motherlode – a huge vein of rich silver ore, some 50 feet long and a foot wide: That's one BIG piece of silver.

Imagine how he must have felt... Out there, all alone in the middle of the Arizona desert, Ed Schieffelin suddenly knew he was a wealthy man:

Remembering his friends' dark jest, Schieffelin staked his claim and named it, "Tombstone."

Other claims rapidly followed Schieffelin's, and in the years that followed, tough hardrock miners pulled some $85 million dollars worth of high-grade silver ore from vast tunnels underneath the city – That's well over a billion dollars in today's currency. To this day it remains the biggest silver strike in Western history.

As if by magic, a "boom town" sprung up on the broad mesa overlooking the Good Enough Mine. A rugged tent city appeared virtually overnight. Streets were quickly mapped out, buildings rose, and were furnished in 1880's finery and equipped for whatever purpose they served, and populated in record time.

Soon, there was a bowling alley, an ice cream parlor, an ice house, two banks, one of the first public swimming pools in Arizona, three newspapers, and a school... ...Oh, and 114 bars, gambling dens, dance halls, and houses of ill repute.

Citizens often dressed themselves in resplendent style; and as the movie correctly states, the latest Paris fashions were sold off the backs of wagons. Store fronts included Kelly's Wine House; which featured 26 different European vintages and Coors beer. The town's main drag, known locally as "wicked Allen Street" was a beehive of activity, 24 hours a day.

A lot of the old, historic town is still surprisingly well-preserved, and the people who live there appreciate its rich history.

The Bird Cage Theater, where Wyatt Earp's friend, Doc Holliday dealt Faro, and Wyatt met entertainer, Josephine Marcus, who he spent the rest of his life with. The Theatre is perfectly preserved – the original place escaped fires and natural disasters and still stands there right on Allen Street, just exactly as it did in the 1880s.

The famous Boot Hill Cemetery is also still there, and so is the old courthouse. The small house where Wyatt Earp actually lived is on Fremont Street – just on the other side of the street from the home of one of the members of the infamous "Cowboys" gang – Pete Spence.

The old mines, which provided the silver that made Tombstone a rip-roaring "boom town" remains as does the OK Corral. But actually, the famous gunfight didn't take place at the OK Corral –

it really took place in a small lot BEHIND the OK Corral, next to Fly's Photography studio, bordering on Fremont Street.

The studio was also the boarding house where Doc Holliday lived. Sadly, it burned down in 1912, but has been faithfully rebuilt. Fires were a big problem in the Old West, because of the combination of all the wood frame buildings and kerosene lanterns and wood stoves, and Tombstone was no exception to the rule.

The old town is still *right there*, still essentially all intact, just as it was back in the 1880s. If Wyatt Earp somehow returned to it today, he'd still recognize the place and know his way around – there's THAT much of it that hasn't changed.

Critics will dismiss the town as a bit "touristy," but those who look deeper will find that its pioneer spirit is alive and thriving. There are tours of the old places, and re-enactors who put on shows and take their authenticity and the town's rich frontier history very seriously; with nice shops and restaurants.

I was interested to find that there were Chinese living there during the 1880s; and that they were not only accepted in Tombstone, but highly respected members of the community... which was pleasing to me –

They called themselves "Celestials" – that's how Chinese were known in the polite form of address of that bygone era. So the Old West, or at least, Tombstone, seems to have been a lot less hostile, and more inclusive and accepting than its "wild-and-wooly" legend would suggest – at least in some ways.

A man named Ah Lum, and his business partner Quang Kee, owned what was acknowledged to be the finest restaurant in town; and Ah Lum's wife, Sing Choy – an astute businesswoman from from Zhongshan Provence, known affectionately as "China Mary," to the townspeople – looked after Tombstone Chinatown's business interests, as a sort of "Godmother" of that community.

From historical accounts she was universally respected by all of Tombstone – Chinese and Anglos alike – not only for her business sense; but also for her honesty, generosity, and kindness. She once took a penniless cowboy with a broken leg to the Grand Central boarding house and paid the medical bills until he had fully recovered.

It was said of her that no injured, sick, or hungry person was ever turned from her door. By all accounts from that era, she was quite a respected and well-beloved member of the community.

So that was an unexpected piece of Tombstone's long and colorful history, that I found fascinating.

After Tombstone, Wyatt and Josephine traveled all over – ranging as far as Alaska, before eventually settling down in Los Angeles, where Wyatt became a technical advisor for the early western movies.

I recently discovered where Wyatt was buried, and so I went there to pay my respects. He's resting in Colma, California, which is up near San Francisco, buried next to Josephine Marcus – the love of his life.

As you can see, I've done my research – I've taken all that energy in, and it's all simmering in my mind.

Eventually my painting will emerge from all that energy that I've taken in:

That's how I do it.

I'm still doing movies, too: MY movies. They're not big, high-dollar, major motion pictures – at least not yet –

Many actors and others in the business look down on that, but then, most of them are still waiting around for years, for that Big Production that's going to make them a household name.

I tell them, "Hey, I'm alive NOW, and I do what I can – At least I'm DOING it." Truthfully, a lot of them can't say as much. At this point in my life, I don't have time to wait around and get discovered for the "Big Break" – I want to get to the point!

Art Camacho, Crystal Santos, Eric

I love to learn new things, and I feel that we should keep learning forever – all our lives. I wonder how many great things that could be gifts to the world don't get done because the people that could do them, DON'T do them, because they've bought into the popular "wisdom" that they're "too old now." I feel that if I'm HERE, I can do it. What do I have to lose by keeping my hand in and staying interested in life?

Beliefs like that are limiting – They consist of what we think is true, but is not necessarily so:

Where is it carved in granite that if you're "old," you have to stop participating fully in life? Why is there a limiting barrier, and is it even true for each and every one of us? How many people don't get out and DO things anymore because they tell themselves that they're "too old?" Is it possible that this attitude might be holding you back from enjoying life to its fullest potential? I think so, and I want to escape that always.

We are all temporary – So what? That's the human condition. While we're here, we're here: So my feeling is, as long as you're here anyway, why not continue living a full life and doing everything you love to do?

> "Eric Lee is a pioneer and maverick in martial arts. He has always taught me to embrace and respect all martial arts. Although his base is in Kung-fu, he infuses the many arts together and in my opinion he ould have an Eric Lee style. He has been one of the best teachers."
>
> -Crystal Santos-Copage, actress and martial artist

We all have a sense of what we can and can't do, physically. If you need to set some limits, fine. But I feel that for myself, those limits should be based on ME, and not on some sort of general, conventional, supposedly age-appropriate "wisdom" that might not be true for me at all.

Those thoughts have weight! They can keep you from doing new things that you'd otherwise like to do if it wasn't for that voice in your head that says, "I'm too old for that!"

There may be real limitations for our personal situation, but I feel it's important to at least consider that perhaps your *belief system* is keeping you old.

If my attitude was "I'm too old for that," I would have missed out on a lot of good things. Nothing ventured, nothing gained, right? What we believe can control our lives in both positive and negative ways. Sometimes we have to let go of limited beliefs to move on to the next level.

As I've said previously, I don't believe in the word "retire." Artistic people don't retire. Why should they? Artists are artists because they do what they love. We know that in a way the *process* is more important than the *result*. I feel that my life is full of adventure, discovery, magic, wonder, and love: Why on earth would anybody want to "retire" from that? That's not good.

It's only good if you've been spending your life doing something that you didn't really like. I like what I do. I'm pretty bold; I'm not afraid to try new things. My philosophy is, "Just do it." Unless you MAKE it happen, nothing happens.

How? I'm a practical person. I like to simplify. I've heard it said that the harder you work, the luckier you get... but I disagree with that a little bit:

It's partially true – It's important to work hard, that's true... But I believe that the SMARTER you work the luckier you get. Not that I'm smarter... but I'm smart enough to know what I don't know. What most people call "luck" involves elements of preparation, knowledge, and information.

So I try to "work smart," and I always do what I say. When I say I'm gonna do it, I do it. Otherwise how can things get done? The saying goes that, "if you talk, the talk, you gotta walk the walk." I always do that. Sometimes I make wrong choices – it happens, who doesn't? If I fail, at least I know what didn't work. When I do make a mistake, I rethink and correct my path, building on

Lady L. Reed , Cindy Daoud, Eric Lee

what I have learned, and the next time, hopefully, it goes a bit smoother: It works for me!

I try to focus on positive things, and I think that's important. Thoughts create feelings and Negative feelings, destructive feelings are not for healing. And that brings us to a VERY important point:

Feeling is an important tool for healing, but as with any "power tool," you have to learn to use your feelings correctly, so that you don't hurt yourself: I've noticed that many people have a tendency to dwell on thoughts they DON'T

"Being Eric's personal assistant is a challenging job, but it's also fun. It's my responsibility to understand a project and handle the details. It can get pretty hectic - I'm on call 24/7. I do it because I like and respect Eric and support his ideals. He's a good-hearted person and that's what counts. I am also a ball of energy, like him – he gets an idea and my job is to do whatever's needed to make it happen. It can be anything... I could be planning all the elements of a massive party, doing social media, organizing trips and flights, solving problems, booking hotels, getting the latest into the newsletter, coordinating projects... I never know quite what's going to be next."

-Rev. Lady Lallaine Reed; certified massage therapist, ordained minister, student of Eric Lee, 4th Degree Tang Soo Do blackbelt, 5th Degree Weikuendo (Leo Fong's student), JKD advance level (Dr. Z), 6 times US National Champion, multiple Hall of Fame Holder, author, editor, actress, dancer.

like – It's important to catch those negative thoughts and chase them away, instead of repeating the "old movie" of our lives all the time, like a bad re-run.

Which reminds me of another famous Chan story...

> Two monks were walking along the road one day, and they came across a beautiful young woman in elaborate silken robes standing at the edge of a huge puddle. The puddle covered the entire road and there was no way around it, so she couldn't cross to get to wherever she was going without ruining her dress.
>
> One of the monks saw her dilemma and without a moment's hesitation said, "Come on, girl!" He picked her up, and carried her across the puddle, and set her down gently on the other side, as the other monk looked on, thoroughly scandalized.
>
> The girl bowed and offered her thanks, and the two monks continued along on their journey, in silence.
>
> That night, the other monk could contain his exasperation no more, so he said to his friend, "you know, as monks, we're not supposed to associate with women. It's not proper! It's just not done! What would people think?!!!"
>
> "I left the girl back there on the road," the monk replied, "are you still carrying her?"

You take that past as part of the chapters of your life – grist for the mill – and you move on. Good or bad, the past is the past and you can't change it, so you have to learn to let it GO: It's where you go from HERE that matters.

Having said that, I find that I often carry a lot more than I should in my mind. I tend to get caught up in all the ideas and projects, I've got going on. My time management is not always as good as it should be, and sometimes I'm not as organized as I would like to be – I'm only human, not perfect. But I accept that nobody's perfect – I don't let the "little things" get in the way of getting it done, or waste time trying to do it all by myself... I'm good at finding talented people who know how to complete their piece of a project, and delegate the tasks that fall within their area of expertise to them. I try to listen carefully to them, and also to "listen between the lines," so that I can understand what they MEAN as well as what they SAY.

My specialty is having the "vision" to see the "Big Picture" clearly and put it all together – like assembling the pieces of a big jigsaw puzzle. Not everybody can do that, but I find that it's easy for me.

I try to be careful not to do too much, but sometimes when my mind gets going, it's hard to relax and shut down all those thoughts that are buzzing around up there... We Chinese call that "monkey brain" – the mind thinking so much that it robs you of your peace of mind.

So I'm learning to work with the traditional beads that the monks use to meditate with, in order to bring all those thoughts under control -   After all, that's what "the pros" use, so I'm learning from their example.

It's not easy, because most of the things that I do are, well, FUN. I genuinely enjoy them.   I find that art CREATES energy rather than takes it, so that makes it harder to put the thoughts down and RELAX.

Business? Business is, well, business... I'm good at business, but it burns energy – for me, it's real work... I find that art CREATES energy, and I naturally prefer that... So I usually schedule the "business" that I have to take care of in the mornings, and once I finish with that chore, I can move on to other things that I like better.

I prefer art. But either one can run your thoughts ragged if you let it.   So whatever you're doing, you have to be able to put it down, and just take a break from it. Otherwise it tries to take over your life.

<u>After all, we work so that we can have a life – not the other way around</u>. If you work for a LIVING, then why kill yourself working? That's not what we're here for; it's not what our human spirit tells us we should be doing. That's just not how nature put us together. We're simply not "wired" to be beasts of burden, or worker bees, any more than a tiger is wired to gather flowers.

So... How to FIND this "better way?" Now that IS a question...

219

The Chinese sage, Lao Tsu, says, "The way to DO is to BE." Hmm... Sounds great as a message in a fortune cookie, but how practical is it, really?

Still... "Do" is a very powerful word. There are few words that are as powerful, in potential, as "do." If you "do" something, other things happen as a consequence. Everybody knows that. Throw a marble into a roomful of mousetraps – action/reaction. Interesting to watch, sure, but so what? But let's go a bit deeper...

If you're Gandhi, and you "do," you free India. If you're Jonas Salk, you cure the world of polio. If you're Leonardo da Vinci, you create timeless works of art and beauty... And the list goes on:

No doubt about it, "do" is powerful.

But our sage, here, is saying MORE than that, isn't he? "Way" in Chinese, is "Tao" - a "path"...Or more loosely translated, a "principle," a "method." So he seems to be talking about a means for taking action in your life...

So maybe, put in modern terms: **"If you REALLY want to get things done, just be yourself."**

Yeah, ok... Sounds good on paper, but how practical is it? Human beings don't exactly come with a manual for self-discovery... And let's face it: A lot of us don't really know who we are, that well. So how do we find out?

I can only tell you what I do, myself. It's actually very simple: I listen to myself. I pay attention to my feelings, and how I react to things. That's my own spirit, telling me things; giving me feedback: I pay close attention to that, and I find a way to follow-up on it!

Each of us finds what fascinate us... things that we like. Things that really capture our attention... Things that we just can't get enough of... When we find one of those things, we don't even have to think about it – we just know it instinctively. *It is written right into our DNA*:

As a "message" there's nothing more personal, more natural, more intimate, than that – When you think about it, that's as personal as it gets, and as close to a "Manual" for Life as you could ask for. And best of all, you don't need a life coach or a self-help book to find it. Just need to pay attention to your own feelings.

Over the years I've systematically built my life around those things, by knowing what I like, recognizing those feelings, and I develop practical ways of being able to do them. As I keep building those pathways I not only get to do what I love, I also build up the practical, entrepreneurial skills that allow me to do them.

It works for me!

So maybe – just maybe – human beings do come with an instruction manual, after all.

There are dreams that we are given to actualize, to bring to life... And good things like honor, respect, and integrity, that make us different from herd animals or beasts of burden...

If we can only devise little, practical ways – not big things at first, but small steps, baby steps, tiny steps leading one-to-the-next – to follow those dreams and work out how to bring them into being in the rocky waters of the real world, there can be better things out there, waiting for us.

Like what? That's up to you! It's up to each of us to discover. I find new things to do all the time. Point A leads to Point B, and so on...

...Like discovering the "Tombstone" story, and going there myself to see what it was like, and sharing it with some friends: That trip will turn into a painting... and a story... and an event, when the painting is sold... and who knows what else? It might be a small thing, it might be a big thing... Not even *I* know, but I'll know it when the idea hits me:

Thus, the marble hits the roomful of mousetraps... That's how I do it.

I've told you, I enjoy jokes. In 2003 I discovered "celebrity roasts" roasts like the old Dean Martin Celebrity Roasts... Well, I say, "discovered" – truthfully I "discovered" it because *I* was "roasted," myself, in 2003, at the Hilton Hotel in Burbank... Five hundred black belts showed up to hear lines like the one about me being this great kata champion... and therefore, one of the world's leading authorities on beating up imaginary people. Now that's funny!

I decided to put on some of those, too. Since then we've roasted a few people like Al Dacascos, and Joycelyne Lew, whom you may remember from the TV series, "Kung Fu." Those events were a lot of fun, and they were well-received, too... So we're definitely going to do more of those. We've got one planned in the near future for tournament superstar and Chuck Norris black belt, John Natividad – Shhhh!!! Don't tell him! It's a secret! :)

I am coming up with other projects to do all the time – big ones, little ones, medium sized ones... simple ones, elaborate ones... I can't help it! I stumble across them all the time, just like Ed Schieffelin did with his silver strike at Goose Flats...

...But I'm very fortunate to have a far easier time of it than Ed Schieffelin did: I don't have to go tramping around on the desert:

I find my treasures in my own mind.

Perhaps you can too.

Steward, Nathan Le Banc, Eric and Scott in Hawaii

Eric & Guro Cocoy Canete

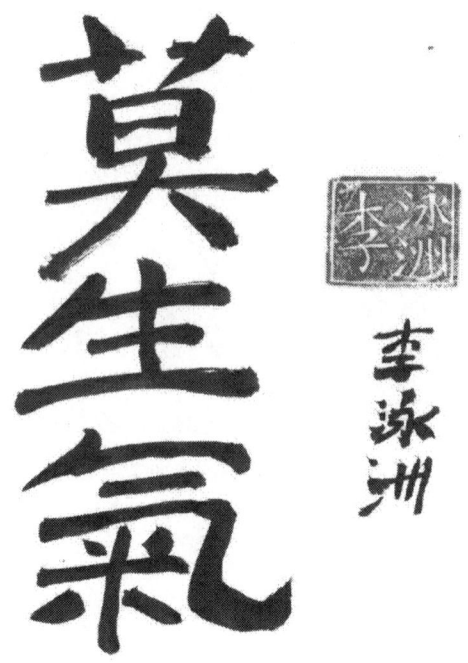

(Don't Waste Your Chi)

"The richness of the human experience would lose something of rewarding joy if there were no limitations to overcome." – Helen Keller

EPILOGUE:

– *"The way to DO, is to BE."* - *Lao Tsu*

So that's my story, the story of my life; my legacy.

That's how I got from Fu Chung Village, Canton, to Los Angeles, California where I live now, what I did in the process of getting there; and a few of the thoughts that occurred to me along the way...

...The story of how "Wing Chow Lee" became "Eric Lee," and how Eric Lee toured the world and became the "Little King of Kata;" and how I moved beyond all that, to just be myself.

That's my story, my thoughts, and my speculations on life. Now they belong to you. It's my sincere hope that somewhere within these ramblings, you may find a jewel or two that's worth cultivating and keeping, to make your own life a bit better.

I wish you well.

Blessings,

Eric Lee

Eric Lee with Cynthia Rothrock and Arnold Schwarzenegger

Having fun with Jackie Chan

Eric Lee and Chuck Norris

With Kurt Russell

Alec Baldwin

Samuel Hong

Bolo Yeung from Enter The Dragon

Steven Seagal from Undersiege

 Benny Urquidez

 Don Wilson

Photo: Eric Lee, Gerald Goldman, Steve Tymon, KW Wong, Murietta Ciavarra, Lady L. Reed, Danny Lopez, Connie Chan, Sgt. Frank Parras Jr., David L. Reed, Mitch Shimer, Kim Marra, Bob Herndon, Joycelyne Lew, Robert Dixon, Bill Perron

Photo: Dan Inosanto, Tino Tuiolosega , Ark Y Wong, Darnell Garcia, John Yee, Douglas Wong, Eric Lee, Daniel Lee

The Calligraphy on each chapter is done by me and I am creating another book full of it.

There are more photographs with many of my friends online. For those whom I didn't include here, please don't get offended. It only means that there were too many shared already. You can access most of them on the following pages.

www.ericlee.com

www.facebook.com/grandmasterericlee

www.youtube.com/gmericlee

Follow me on Instagram #gmericlee

LinkedIn Grandmaster Eric Lee

Made in the USA
Coppell, TX
16 January 2026

67280212R00129